PRECIOUS HONORED LOVED

Journey to The Greater Life

LOUISE MUELLER

Printed in the United States of America

ISBN: 9798327249745

Independently published

Cover Photo, Design, and Art:
William Fridrich and Marsha McKee

This book is dedicated to those wanting to know who they really are.

CONTENTS

ACKNOWLEDGMENTS

Thanks to God for showing me this journey to
The Greater Life. You're the best!

Thank you, Jim Mueller, for your love and support.
You mean so much to me.

Thanks to my friends whom God used to teach
and guide me along the way.
I couldn't have done it without you.

Thanks to all those who encouraged me to keep writing
by commenting on my blog.
Thank you, Stefanie Shotton, for checking my blogs
before each posting.
You are all appreciated more than you know.

1 ACCEPTANCEVILLE

I'd come a long way with all the lessons on love. My view of a lot of things was changing, and because of it, I'd become more loving and compassionate. In Acceptanceville, it was all turned up a notch when a side lesson, while studying the gospel of Luke, showed me some of what I hadn't been seeing. It changed my outlook on life and how I viewed myself and others.

It started with something I read in our weekly lesson that challenged me. Jesus said in Luke 6:37, "Do not judge, and you will not be judged." I didn't take it as that God would judge me; I already knew I had been forgiven through faith in what Jesus did on the cross. But I was looking for a better life here on earth, so I took it to mean, "Do not judge, and you will not be judged by others." It got me wondering if I had something to do with the criticism that had come my way. Had I somehow brought it on by judging others? I didn't know how it all worked exactly, but I was at the point where I was willing to find out. So, trusting Jesus, I started looking at my thoughts.

At first, whenever I would notice a judgmental thought, I would stop and call it what it was. *That's a judgmental thought,* I would think to myself. Just interrupting the thought that way would often cause it to go away. The more I recognized my judgmental thoughts, especially those about others, the more I felt bad for thinking them and wanted to change. So, I decided that whenever I noticed a judgmental thought, I would change it to something more positive. If I saw something I didn't like about someone, I would immediately try to find something I liked about them. At a certain point, it occurred to me that it took some judgment to determine a good thought from a bad one. So, for a while, I tried to chase away all judgmental thinking. Then, I remembered that in the beginning, God judged everything as "good." That's when I decided that "good" thoughts could stay. Slowly, my thoughts changed from negative to positive, from critical to complimentary. That's when I felt myself searching for the good in people and in situations instead of always first looking for what's wrong. I started seeing more of what was right and good in everything.

From there, I began to see how I had been judging everything according to what I thought it should be. Then, one day, while reviewing some artwork with a client, I noticed something he said quite often. Whenever there was something that couldn't be changed, something that needed to be there in a specific place and size, my client would say, "It is what it is." Thinking about it later, I thought, *What a great way of accepting things as they are.* I liked it and decided to adopt it for myself.

Later, I thought, *Why can't I apply that same phrase to people too?* People are what they are. Who am I to try to change them? I started to think that by judging someone, I was trying to make them into what I wanted them to be. When I couldn't get them to fit into what I thought they should be, I'd get frustrated, and conflicts would always follow. I started to see how much people don't like feeling judged; it makes them mad. It makes me mad. And it makes me feel bad about myself like there's something wrong with me. That's when I realized that we all want to be accepted for who we are, and it hurts when we aren't.

Laying down my judgmental thoughts allowed me

to begin accepting people and things the way they are, but something else changed, too. My guilt and inadequacies faded, and I began to accept myself. Instead of being focused on the weaknesses of others, my eyes began to open to their uniqueness and what I could learn from them and enjoy. I was also more able to see their needs and how I could possibly help them. I started to view everyone as a forgiven child of God, whether they realized they were or not. I began to see that everyone has potential, whether they display it or not. And once I started to see it in others, I couldn't help but see it in myself.

After accepting myself for who I am, I noticed a change I hadn't expected. I didn't feel the need to compete or compare myself with others as much. There didn't seem to be any reason to defend myself, if only in my own eyes. Everyone and everything became friendlier. I discovered how much fun it is to help, encourage others, and work together to bring about good. A lot of what I had been frustrated with, to the point of anger, seemed to change on its own, and most of the time, I was the one who ended up changing.

No longer seeing things as an enemy, or something that needed to be changed, allowed me to see how things really are instead of how I thought they should be. More importantly, I noticed that I was limiting everything I saw by looking at things as I thought they should be. Judging things through only my knowledge and understanding kept my life to only what I knew. Not judging opened me up to the greater possibilities that I didn't know and couldn't see. My life began to open, enlarge, and brighten.

There were so many lessons in Acceptanceville, each changing how I viewed life in ways I could never have anticipated. The truth is, I never would have found my way there if I hadn't first just done what Jesus said to do. It's not something I could have understood unless I had experienced it myself. It's almost like the very thing I was to overcome there was the thing that kept me from finding my way there in the first place. It was there all along, but I couldn't see it. Some of the stuff Jesus says is not easy to understand. That's why the most valuable lesson from my journey through Acceptanceville was letting go of my need to understand everything upfront. I learned that if I just do what Jesus says to do, I'll begin to understand in a whole new way. Seeing all that I got out of that one act of obedience has made me want to trust Jesus to an even greater extent so I can see even greater possibilities. I'm excited to see what they will be.

2 OPPORTUNITYVILLE

On my journey, God had been getting His messages to me at church and through books, songs, and other people. Though I seemed to recognize when it was from God, I wanted to be able to hear from Him more directly. I was also wanting increased faith. Both of those desires were answered, quite amazingly, in Opportunityville.

It all started one Sunday morning at church while greeting when one of my favorite associate pastors asked me if Jim and I would be interested in taking a 10-week leadership class. He briefly explained that the class would be taught by him, our head pastor at the time, and their wives. They were offering biblical leadership principles, hoping to train future leaders for small group Bible studies. He asked me to talk it over with Jim and then let him know our decision.

It turned out Jim wasn't as interested in it as I was. He actually had no interest in being a group leader. The thought of being a group leader scared me, but I was excited about the opportunity to learn and spend time each week with these pastors. For some reason, I thought my faith would increase just by being exposed to people I thought had great faith. Jim may have eventually gone along because I wanted to, but he was out once we found out the class was being held on our bowling night. I struggled with it, though. As much as I enjoyed bowling and that time with Jim and the others on our team, I was having a hard time passing up the opportunity to learn and grow from the pastors I admired so much. It all went back and forth in my mind until a single thought made it very clear what my decision should be—*Could I put bowling above God?*

The thought of putting bowling above God sounded really silly to me. I could tell that Jim wasn't happy about the idea of me taking 10 weeks off from bowling, yet he did encourage me to go ahead on my own if I wanted. How would my teammates feel about it, though? I didn't know but decided to discuss it with them before telling the pastor I would take the class. The following day, I woke up remembering something—the invitation was for Jim and me. If Jim didn't take the class, did it mean I couldn't either? I wondered. So, I emailed the question to the pastor. He replied that couples need to grow together. I had already noticed that Jim and I seemed to be growing at a different pace. The thought that it could cause a problem in our marriage hadn't occurred to me. As much as I wanted to grow in faith, I certainly wouldn't want to hurt what Jim and I had together.

There was no way I was going to talk Jim out of bowling. Besides, there was also the financial aspect to consider. Even though we wouldn't be bowling, we would still be responsible for the weekly league fees. I was willing to bear it, but it would be expensive for both of us. There was so much adding up against this opportunity that I finally concluded that we should wait until the next time they offer the class and hope it's on a different night of the week.

After deciding, I bowled a 200-game Tuesday night with 5 strikes in a row! I couldn't help but take it as confirmation that I had made the right decision. I also shared with our teammates what I had been considering. I hadn't thought they'd be happy, but their reaction surprised me. They were upset that I didn't have the same level of commitment to our team that they had. Although I could see their point, I still thought I shouldn't let it interfere with what God had for me to do. After talking with them, I was glad I had already decided.

Disappointed, I shared the story with my new Bible study group leader during a get-to-know-you lunch. I told her about the opportunity and how I wanted to take the class, not so much to be a group leader but to be around people of great faith. She told me that putting my faith in people wasn't a good idea and that I should always look to Jesus. When I heard her say it, I knew she was right. That night, I had trouble sleeping. What we talked about kept going through my mind, and I felt bad when I realized I had been putting a person of great faith between me and God. So, I told God I was sorry and that I was going to give up the idea.

The following day, I woke up to a couple of thoughts that seemed to be speaking to me. The first thought said, *You step into that position.* Not knowing what the thought was referring to, I said, "What?!" Immediately came another thought: *You be that person of great faith you are looking for.* Right away, I knew it was God speaking to me. I knew because the idea of me being that person is something I wouldn't have thought of. But it did seem like something God would have. Then, in my mind, I saw myself step forward. My left foot stepped into the person of great faith, and my right foot stepped into the leadership position.

Sunday at church, while I was greeting, the pastor came to talk to me again. I explained our conflict with the schedule and that although I would be willing to skip bowling for the 10 weeks, Jim was not. Then he told me I could attend the class alone if I wanted. By then, I was already at peace with my decision, thinking God had confirmed and blessed it with the 200 game I bowled. And so, I told him we'd wait for the next class.

Even though the opportunity didn't work out, I had learned so much through the decision process that I wondered if I had grown more than if I had taken the class. Again, I had been caught trying to get something through my own means instead of going to God with it. When I finally did, not only did God speak to me directly, but His telling me to be that person of great faith must have meant He thought that I could be. And that thought increased my faith greatly. Still, I didn't feel ready to be a leader; more on that next.

3 PROMISEVILLE

While in pursuit of great faith, I found myself wanting to better understand God's promises and how they could help me in my life. Even more so, I tried to understand why I didn't always get what was promised. One reason was illustrated for me when the verse I was to memorize for my Bible study lesson came to life during a walk through Promiseville.

While walking with my husband, Jim, and our dog, Sandy one Sunday afternoon, I was reciting Luke 11:9 over and over again. "Ask, and it will be given to you; seek and you will find; knock, and the door will be opened to you." Besides wanting to be able to recite it from memory for my next class, I also wanted to understand if it was supposed to be three separate promises or if it was a progression of persistence, as asked in the lesson.

As I tried to work it out in my mind, hoping it would eventually all make sense, we came up behind a man walking really slowly. He was so slow that I assumed he had some disability. As we passed by him, I said, "Hello." Then I heard him yell at us and ask, "Where is Sunkist School?" I yelled back to him, saying, "It's in the other direction, a few blocks down." But the man waved us on like he didn't believe me and said, "Oh, that's okay, I'll find it."

As we continued walking, I questioned what the man had said. I couldn't understand why he would ask where the school was, ignore the answer, and continue in the wrong direction. How did he think he would find it, I wondered. Then, the memory verse came to my mind again. I thought, *What if you ask like that man did but then reject the answer? How will you find?* I remembered the question in our lesson about it possibly being a progression. At the time, I thought of it as separate steps of faith: first, you ask; if you don't get an answer, you seek; if you don't find, then you knock. But the verse said you WILL find, which started me wondering about all the times I thought I didn't get answers. Could I have actually been given the answer but didn't recognize it, or ignored it because it wasn't the answer I expected, or didn't trust it, and that's why

I didn't find it? That man sure gave me a different way to think about it, and it got me thinking he may have been an angel sent to help me understand the verse.

As we started our way home, I noticed the man again. This time, he was standing up against a tree and seemed to be holding onto it. As we passed, I asked him, "Are you alright?" He answered, "No, I'm in pain and need help." *Uh oh,* I thought, *he must not be an angel after all.* So, we backed up and asked the man how we could help him.

He said he was having trouble walking but wanted to get home, which was a few blocks down the street. He thought he could make it if we walked with him and held onto him. So, Jim held onto the man, I took Sandy's leash, and we all walked toward where he said he lived. Slowly, at a snail's pace, we walked. We hadn't gotten very far when I suggested we go and get our car. The man kept insisting he could make it, but at this rate, I thought it would take the rest of the day and into tomorrow. When he finally agreed, we decided Jim would be faster at getting the car. So, Sandy went with Jim, and I stayed with the man.

The man and I talked as we continued walking. Polite chit-chat at first; he told me his name was Bud, and I told him mine. Before I knew it, we got into quite an interesting conversation when Bud looked at me and said, "What you must think of me." Without thinking, I told him, "Oh, you'd be surprised at what I thought of you." He didn't say anything but looked curious like he really wanted to know. At that point, I was tempted to change the subject out of fear of what he might think of me, but something in me wanted to tell him the truth. So, I bravely said, "I thought you were an angel sent from God." Then he got a strange, puzzled look on his face like he must not have heard me right. So, I recited the memory verse for him and explained that I thought he was an angel from God sent to help me understand it more fully. After telling him the whole story, I asked if he believed in God. He told me he believed in a supreme being. He said that he believed in the "signs," that he was a Capricorn, and that Jesus was also.

Finally, Jim came with the car. It was a good thing he did because Bud had some trouble remembering exactly how to get to his house. After pointing us down a few streets, we did happen to find his house. Jim pulled into the driveway; immediately, I jumped out of the car and knocked on the front door.

When his wife came to the door, she was angry, yelling that he had left more than two hours ago to get chicken, and where was it, she asked. I tried to tell her he wasn't feeling well and should be checked out by a doctor, but she didn't seem concerned. She said it wasn't the first time someone had to bring him home. She yelled at him, asking how many he'd had and where he had left the car. She seemed more concerned about the car than about him. We told her we didn't know where the car was and left them arguing.

As we drove away, there was so much going through my mind. I was so surprised at how it had turned out. How'd I not catch on that Bud was drunk, I wondered. It's not like I hadn't seen people in that condition before. I also thought how amazing it was that my Bible study had come to life; we asked, sought, knocked, and got Bud home! I felt good that I had the courage to share the memory verse with Bud. I prayed that he would remember it and that it would help him somehow. And later, it occurred to me that the car was probably at Sunkist School.

4 REWARDVILLE

I'd come a long way, learning in different areas of my life. With still much to learn, as my journey continued, I'd be introduced to new concepts and led back through some areas in order to gain a deeper understanding. In Rewardville, a slight shift in perspective revealed more about love and showed me that it's not without rewards.

It started with a nice dinner at a friend's house. After dinner, all I wanted to do was go home and enjoy a glass of wine on the patio as the sun went down. But as we were coming in the door, the phone was ringing. It was my mom wanting me to come over and take her to the store to get a loaf of bread. As much as I tried to get her to say it could wait until tomorrow, she wasn't budging. Finally, Jim said he would go. Even though he didn't know about my plan, I couldn't help feeling guilty about enjoying myself while he cared for my mom. So, I decided to go with him, thinking we could make it a quick trip and then return home to relax.

It turned out to be more than a quick trip. When we got to my mom's house, she was stressed out, frantically searching for her credit card. She had looked all through her purse and was in the process of checking the pockets of the clothes she had recently worn. So, Jim and I joined in the search, which included calling the restaurant where we had dinner a couple of nights before.

When we finally got home, I decided to go ahead and have the glass of wine I had looked forward to earlier. I first took it into the living room, but an idea came to me as I was about to sit down on the couch. Even though it was dark, it was a nice evening, and there wasn't any reason not to enjoy my wine on the patio as I had initially planned. Shortly after I got out there, I heard the Disneyland fireworks start up. We hear the fireworks from Disneyland every night but usually can't see them through all the trees in our neighborhood. That night, though, for some reason, I decided to stroll around our backyard while facing the direction of the sound. That's when I found one tiny spot where I could stand and see the tops of the fireworks in between the trees, and I was thrilled!

Thinking about it the next morning, I realized I had been given something even better than I had initially planned—fireworks! I felt like I had been rewarded for doing the right thing, even though I didn't do it with the best attitude. I started to feel bad about how I had treated my mom. I'd been trying to respond to her needs patiently, but last night, I felt like I had reverted to my selfish self. Yet, it didn't make sense for me to give up something I really wanted for something I thought could have waited until the next day. When my mom disagreed, I felt controlled, which is what seemed to bother me the most. Even though I did what my mom wanted, I resented it and, like in the past, blamed her for not getting my way. This time was a little different, though. This time, I could see where I went wrong and didn't continue in my unhappiness as long as I used to.

Later, I received an even greater understanding when it occurred to me that it wasn't really the bread my mom wanted that night. It was reassurance that although she could still live independently, she was not alone. That's when I realized that the weird demands my mom sometimes made were not to control me but were instead a way of asking for something she may not have known at the time she needed—love.

Seeing everything from this new perspective made me sad about my mom being alone. Most of the time, she seemed happy to still be living independently. As happy as I was about it, I was now beginning to see how afraid it must have made her to call me and get into an argument instead of what she really needed. Once I understood that simply responding to my mom's requests would make her feel loved and secure, I was much more patient with her. I no longer felt coerced into doing something out of duty or responsibility; instead, I began to see it as my choice to show my mom some love.

Fireworks light up the sky every night over Disneyland, but seeing them that night in Rewardville was visible proof that God was looking out for me. It showed me that I didn't have to give up what I wanted out of life to care for my mom. Learning to trust God with my desires has made for some fun surprises. It also enabled me to do much more than I could have imagined, as my mom became increasingly dependent on me as time went on.

5 ZACCHAEUSVILLE

As a child, I was taught right from wrong and given rules, not knowing they were basically the Ten Commandments. Throughout my journey, I'd been trying even harder to do the right thing, thinking that's what God wanted. So, when I was first introduced to the idea of leaving the law behind and continuing under grace, it didn't make much sense to me until two stories from my Bible lesson and a special moment with my mother indicated that was where the road to great faith was headed.

Something about the rich young ruler and Zacchaeus in the gospel of Luke got my attention. With the two stories just a chapter apart, I couldn't help but notice that both men had an encounter with Jesus yet went away with very different results.

The young ruler, in chapter eighteen, asked Jesus

what he must do to inherit eternal life. Jesus went over the law with him, and the man said he had kept it since he was a boy. He must have thought he was doing good until Jesus told him to do something he wasn't able to do. Jesus told him to sell everything he had, give it to the poor, and follow Him. The Bible says the young ruler went away sad.

The next chapter tells of a man named Zacchaeus who, wanting to get a look at Jesus through the crowd, climbed a tree in Jesus' path. When Jesus came by, He called for Zacchaeus to come down and told him He must stay at his house. The Bible says Zacchaeus welcomed Jesus gladly and ended up giving half his possessions to the poor and promised to pay back fourfold those he had defrauded. And Jesus said salvation had come to his house.

After reading the two stories, I didn't quite understand it all, but I saw a clear difference between God's law and grace. The rich young ruler followed the law and did everything right his entire life but didn't get eternal life. Yet, Zacchaeus, who spent his life swindling people, ended up with salvation. It didn't seem right, but I somehow knew there was more in the two stories for me to learn.

The next morning, the stories were still on my

mind. I thought about Zacchaeus and how the Bible says he received Jesus gladly. I wasn't sure that would be my feelings if Jesus suddenly told me He was staying at my house. I'd be wondering if my house was clean, not to mention what I'd do about dinner. And, if I were to be honest, I don't think it would be easy for me to give everything I had to the poor. So, could that be the lesson? Was I still trying to make myself worthy of God's love even after all I've learned on my journey? I already knew I was saved by grace and not by anything I could do. I knew that God loved me just as I am, and it's made an amazing difference in my life. And, I'd put together that I can do more with God than I could ever imagine before knowing God. So, what were these two stories trying to tell me? I wondered.

Later, I realized they answered a question I'd had for some time. I had often wondered how I could have accepted Christ, attended church every Sunday, and still had come to the point of planning to kill myself. I never understood how that could happen, but through the two stories, I realized it was because I hadn't yet experienced God. I saw that after Jesus went home with Zacchaeus and spent time with him, he could do what the young ruler couldn't do. That's when I realized the difference in my life had also come through my relationship with Jesus. On this journey, God became real to me in a way no one can talk me out of, and when I came to know that God loves me just the way I am, that made such a difference in my feelings of worthiness.

As happy as I was to have finally found meaning in the two Bible stories, some additional understanding came through a conversation with my mother a couple days before Christmas. Feeling stressed over all that needed to be done to prepare for the holiday, my mother read me her list while we sat at her kitchen table. After each thing, I told her I had taken care of it. As she continued, I told her, "Don't worry, Mom, I have it all taken care of. All you have to do is appreciate it." After hearing myself say it, I had one of those "light bulb" moments and made an "aha" sound out loud. My mother heard it and said, "What?" I was afraid to tell her because it was about God, and she was already tired of hearing me talk so much about Him. Having to tell her something, I decided to be honest and tell her the truth. So, I said, "I was thinking that could be what God wants to say to us all the time. Don't worry, I've taken care of everything. All you have to do is appreciate it." To my surprise, she nodded in agreement.

The conversation with my mom turned out to be a

special moment with her. Still, I wondered if I'd missed something in Zacchaeusville. I thought about how my mom didn't know what I'd already done for her, and it made me wonder if these stories were telling me there were things Jesus did for me that I didn't know about. Finally, understanding that I could give up trying to make myself feel worthy of God's love just by accepting what Jesus did for me when He fulfilled the law, brought me to a place of gratitude I had never been before. But could there be even more, I wondered.

Making my way through Zacchaeusville, I somehow knew the lessons on grace were only beginning. All indications were that I'd gone as far as possible with God's law, and it was time to learn more about God's grace. I didn't know where grace would take me, but I was excited to learn more about what Jesus did for me and how it works in my life.

6 RADICALVILLE

I had been reading books on radical faith about people who had stepped out with God to do amazing things. As my faith grew, I was anxious to try it out and see what it could do. I even told God I wanted to get out of the boat, so to speak, and walk on water. But when the opportunity presented itself, I didn't recognize it, and a new set of tests, trials, and lessons on my journey with God began.

When the teaching director at Community Bible Study called to inform me that I had been recommended to be a children's Bible teacher for the following year, I couldn't help but laugh. The idea of me being a children's teacher seemed so ridiculous that I told her there must be some mistake. Quickly, she checked her records, asked me my name, and then said, "No, no mistake." After explaining to her that I had no teaching experience, no children, and hadn't been a Christian all that long, I thought it would obviously end the conversation. Instead, she informed me that they had a training program and further shared that they are a praying bunch, indicating it was no accident I'd been recommended, and if by chance there had been a mistake, my name would not have made it through the many prayer sessions before being called. She then asked me to pray about it, to pay attention to pertinent scripture that comes to me, and to let her know my decision in a few days. I told her I would. So, I prayed, and before I knew it, I was calling to tell her I'd do it, only thinking it was a test of my faith that would be called off at the next step.

The next step in the process was a get-to-know-you luncheon given by the director and leadership team for all the new leaders. On the way to the luncheon, a song on the radio got my attention. I'd heard it many times before but hadn't noticed how it started until that moment. It began with the words, "You and I must make a pact. We must bring salvation back." The song continued, "Where there is love, I'll be there. I'll reach out my hand to you. I'll have faith in all you do. Just call my name, and I'll be there." It was the song "I'll Be There" sung by Michael Jackson, but it felt like God was speaking to me. Was this song God's way of telling me the teacher idea was from Him? I wondered.

The luncheon was lovely, and being around all those ladies of faith was inspiring. After we ate, the teaching director told us a little about herself and then asked us to take turns going around the table, each sharing something. I found it interesting that the director of the children's ministry didn't have any children either. I was touched when she said, "But I feel like I have a hundred children." As much as it all seemed to be pointing me toward accepting the position, there was still time for it to be called off. The interview with the teaching director, where I would be expected to commit my time two mornings a week for 8 months, wasn't for a couple of weeks.

During my Bible study group the following week, I was given another, even more powerful, reason for accepting the position. It came while reading the verse in the gospel of Luke where Jesus told the disciples to let the children come to Him. That's when I felt the Lord say to me, "If you tell a child about Me, then that child won't have to go through life without Me like you did." I knew it wasn't something I would have thought. And if it was God, how could I ignore such a thought?

Losing hope that it would be called off, I started taking the idea more seriously as the interview with the teaching director approached. As scary and unlikely as it was that I could somehow be a children's Bible teacher, at the same time, I wanted to trust and follow God. So, with just a couple of hours left before the interview, I prayed, "Lord, I know I shouldn't ask this when You've already given me two powerful answers, but I need one more confirmation to be sure it's from You."

The morning of the interview was my group's turn to serve in the children's department. Although it was my second time that year to assist a teacher in a classroom, this was a chance to picture myself as the teacher and get a feel for if I would like it. Right away, I got involved with the kids, playing games, and helping with their crafts. One little boy didn't want to do what the teacher had planned. While the other kids sang songs and recited their memory verses, he was going around pinching them. After many attempts to get the boy to stop, the teacher asked me to take him to the children's director.

So, I took hold of his little hand and walked toward the table where I knew to find the children's director. Silently, I sympathized with him, thinking it must feel like being sent to the principal's office. With the tables in sight, the boy began talking. As I knelt down to listen, he told me he had trouble settling down because the video games he played before class were still going through his head. Wow, I couldn't help but think that was important information he had shared with me. So, I tried to help him by asking, "What if you focused on what the teacher was saying? Do you think all the video game stuff might go away?" He nodded yes as we continued toward the tables. When we got there, though, no one was there. As I reached to open the gate to check the playground, I felt a tug on my hand. The boy told me he would be good if I took him back to class. "You'll concentrate on your lesson and do what the teacher says?" I asked. After promising, we returned to class just in time for me to head over to my interview.

On my way to meet the teaching director, I couldn't help but think the experience with the boy was the one additional confirmation I had prayed for. It showed me that I could handle the children with God there. As I walked into the interview, I still had difficulty committing, even with the three strong reasons I'd been given for taking the position. *What if I didn't like it? It would be a really long year,* I was thinking. Then, the director happened to say the only words that would relieve my fear enough to make the commitment. She said, "Why don't you get started, and if you don't like it, come tell me, and we'll find you something else."

7 ANOINTVILLE

Although the idea that I could somehow be a children's Bible teacher made no sense, it was clear that God had led me there. Never in my life could I ever remember feeling so unprepared, but I'd made up my mind to trust God. Preparation began, mainly in the style much of my journey had already—by changing my thinking, but in a way I hadn't yet experienced. In Anointville, I was to be shown how the power of God can enable me to do what I didn't think I could.

The interview where I'd finally accepted the position went a little long, causing the teaching director to hurry downstairs to begin her lecture on time. While in the elevator, she put her hand on my shoulder and said the most amazing prayer. Hearing her ask God for my anointing was a special moment I'll always treasure. It also made it all so much more real.

This is really happening, I thought. At the same time, it reminded me of what I'd heard her say many times, "God doesn't call the equipped; He equips the called," and whatever I needed to effectively teach the children would come from God. And it started coming before the year was done.

All year, my leader had been reminding our group about sharing day—the last day of class when we were to share at the potluck brunch something we'd learned from the study that year. I didn't want to disappoint my leader, but the thought of getting up in front of the entire group of ladies and speaking into a microphone made me nervous. I didn't know if I'd be able to do it. With the day fast approaching, I still wasn't sure what to share until the answer to a prayer came to me while at a baseball game with friends.

My prayer was for a nice singing voice. Ever since I was told by an elementary school music teacher that I was tone deaf, I've avoided singing or sang at whisper volume so no one could hear me. I'm sure my prayer was also prompted by knowing how much of a role singing plays in the children's ministry and the thought that as a teacher next year, I'd be the lead singer.

One of the verses we were to memorize during the

year was Luke 11:9, "Ask and it will be given to you; seek and you will find; knock and the door will be opened to you." I didn't see any reason why God couldn't give me a nice singing voice if I asked Him. So, I asked. I also made it my prayer request for the week, enlisting the ladies in my group to join me in praying. When my voice hadn't changed, I began to wonder why.

Then, while at the baseball game, the answer came to me, only not as I had expected. During the seventh inning stretch, a six-year-old boy was introduced to lead the traditional singing of "Take Me Out to the Ball Game." In front of thousands of people, the boy stood up to the microphone and sang with glee. As I found myself singing along and thinking I couldn't sound any worse than he did, the answer came to me. If that kid could inspire me to sing with him, maybe others around me during worship who, like me, are uncomfortable with their voice might be inspired to sing when they hear me. So, the answer was not to be given a different voice but to instead change how I thought about the voice I had been given. That was what I wanted to share.

I'd written it out and practiced it so much that I had it almost memorized. Yet, I couldn't get through it without crying, which made me even more nervous.

So, I prayed, "Lord, please don't let me cry in front of all those people." Even with all the practice and prayers, I didn't think I could share my story when the day came. During lunch, my leader curiously asked if I was going to share. I told her I wasn't sure and headed to the restroom. While in there, I talked with myself and somehow managed to muster up enough courage to get in line for the microphone. I prayed while waiting for my turn. When I heard the woman in front of me speaking into the microphone, my heart skipped a beat. It not only meant that I was next, but she was crying and having trouble continuing, which brought back my biggest fear. So, I went back to praying, this time for her. I prayed she would have the strength to finish what she wanted to share. It turned out she was able to finish, and then she passed the microphone to me.

Nervously, I introduced myself and began sharing; "Luke 11:9 was the only verse I was able to memorize because I feel my relationship with God has grown based on that promise." As I recited the verse, a peace seemed to come over me. I felt at ease as I continued, even through the part that had usually made me cry: "Asking God my questions and having the answers show up in different ways has made God real to me in a way no one can talk me out of. It has strengthened my faith and told me that God loves me in a way nothing else could." It seemed very quiet in the room when I got to: "Yet when the question came up in our group about why we don't always get what we ask for, I didn't have a confident answer. So, I asked God." As I shared about how I had asked for a nice singing voice and my change in thinking that came as a result, I hadn't anticipated the gasp that would come from the children's teachers when I said I couldn't have sounded any worse than the boy did at the ball game. Quickly, my hand went up to calm them until I could finish my point. The applause made me feel good, but I was relieved when I was done and a little surprised it wasn't as bad as I had anticipated all those weeks.

I still believe God could miraculously give me a nice singing voice, but learning that He could somehow use the voice I had already seemed more valuable for the time. Though I'm really glad God didn't have me sing to the ladies at the brunch, pressing through my insecurities and having the courage to tell my story in that way relieved my fear of singing to the children. Sensing God's power in Anointville encouraged me to follow God further into unfamiliar territory. While preparation continued preparing me for the children in the fall, I'd be shown other capabilities I had unwisely judged about myself. I'll share more about that next.

8 LEADERVILLE

Along with the children's Bible teacher position came the privilege of being included in the leaders' group. Even though I didn't see myself as a leader, the thought of studying the Bible with a group of women who put their faith into action serving the Lord excited me. The title didn't seem to fit me, though. I'd always thought of myself as independent-minded. I enjoyed doing my own thing and the freedom of not being responsible for anyone but me. Over the summer vacation, something changed how I saw myself, which prepared me to lead the children in a way I could never have planned.

It so happened that our church was hosting the Chick-fil-A Leadercast. I signed up for the seminar thinking it might help prepare me to be a good leader. It turned out to be geared toward business leadership, but I saw that some information could be applied to managing children. Looking back at the notes I took, which were few, three of the points turned out to be key in teaching the children. They were: "Creativity = putting imagination into practice," "Innovation = putting great ideas into practice," and "Enjoy, not just endure." Being a graphic designer, I could easily relate to the first two points. The third point was a little more challenging but still ended up playing a crucial role in my first year of the children's ministry and also helped me journey through caring for my mother.

The seminar was wonderfully planned, with video interviews of successful people sharing their wisdom and illustrated with lots of practical experiences. I was so impressed with how the material was presented that I wondered if my next purpose might be in seminar presentations. As I listened and tried to absorb what I could from the information offered, there was much that didn't seem to apply to me until a woman shared a story about mountain climbing. When she started, I thought, *That's something I would never do.* I was tempted to daydream instead. I was really glad that I didn't because the lesson she shared, intermingled with climbing up the steepest part of the mountain, was what stuck with me most from the entire seminar.

The lesson came as she shared details of what she called “hitting the wall.” She described it as a place where you feel like you’ve gone as far as you can. Thinking you can’t go any farther, you’re tempted to turn back without reaching the top and finishing your goal. She told of how when she had gotten to that point in her climb, others on their way back down the mountain encouraged her to keep going. They told her how beautiful it was at the top and how much it was worth the struggle getting there. Encouraged, she continued with tiny little steps. One tiny step at a time was all she could do, but it moved her forward, and she had made it to the top before she knew it. I wasn’t sure how that story would make me a leader, but I somehow knew it was an important lesson to remember.

Another lesson came while on vacation that suddenly changed how I thought of myself. It happened in the Minneapolis airport when Jim and I were returning home from visiting my aunt and cousin. We had also played golf in North Dakota, checking off the last Midwest state left for us to play in our goal of playing all fifty. While waiting in line to check in, a man came and drew the ribbon in front of me, closing off the line. Pointing, he instructed me to go to my left. As I walked that way, I could see how far

I had to go through the maze of ribbons connected to poles and would end up back where I was, only on the other side of the ribbon. So, I decided to duck under the ribbon to save myself a few steps. That's when I heard the man yell, "I knew that was coming!" When I looked back, I saw that my husband had followed me, which I had expected, but to my surprise, I saw the entire line behind us ducking under the ribbon. Then loudly, the man said, pointing to me, "And she started this whole thing!" As embarrassing as it was, at that moment, I saw that I was a leader whether I realized it or not. People were following me, so the only question was, what kind of leader would I be?

Later, I realized that everyone was forced to follow me or lose their place in line. As smart as I thought I was, I had made the airport employee's job a lot harder. With all the confusion I had caused that day, also came a clarity that showed me that, as independent as I thought I once was, my actions were affecting others. As I began to feel a greater responsibility for my actions and the example I showed others, I became even more determined to look to God for instructions. With each step I took through Leaderville came the instructions and encouragement I needed to continue moving forward when the going got tough.

9 TEACHERVILLE

The road to great faith taught me that with God, I'm capable of doing far more than I ever thought possible. Though teaching children about Jesus seemed too far out of my comfort zone, the time had come to put what I'd learned into action and see what my faith could do. Lessons leading into Teacherville had prepared me mentally, and the day of practical training I'd been promised was about to begin. Still, it seemed so strange; in a week, I'd announce to a class of four-year-olds that I was their teacher. I couldn't help wondering what I was doing there, but my doubts were answered with reassurance that God had brought me there and was there with me. I would also be given an incredible surprise gift that would turn my insecurities into fun.

Training Day had finally come. I felt nervous and excited as I waited with the leaders and other children's teachers for the teaching director to arrive and begin the day. Silently, I prayed and asked God to teach me to be a teacher. I told Him I had emptied myself and asked Him to fill me with everything I needed. My prayer was interrupted by sudden silence when a man entered the room, an unusual sight for this organization of women. He announced that he was our teaching director's husband and explained that his wife was in Intensive Care with a life-threatening condition. We all bowed our heads in prayer. After the prayer, the man left, and the meeting continued under the leadership of the assistant teaching director from the previous year.

This was like no place I'd been before. Looking around the room, I thought, *I can learn much from these women.* After an announcement like that, I'd expected the meeting to be dismissed and rescheduled for later. That's what would usually happen in business after such news. But this meeting continued, delayed only by the announcement and a prayer. There was no bickering, no discussion of who should be in charge. And from an organization of volunteers where no one gets paid, I was impressed.

When it came time to introduce myself to the other children's teachers, I admitted I hadn't any teaching experience, not even children of my own. I didn't know what I was doing there, but I was trusting God. Their reaction was not what I had expected. They seemed inspired by my faith and went to work explaining lesson plans and gathering everything I needed for my first day of class. At the end of the day, I had a fun box of supplies that included crayons, playdough, glue sticks, and other stuff I hadn't played with since I was a kid. Later, as I carried it to my car, I was feeling overwhelmed with all the information from the day and felt like running away. Driving out of the church parking lot, the song "I'll Be There" by Michael Jackson came on the radio just as it had when I first decided whether or not to take the position. I smiled when I heard it, knowing God was letting me know He was there with me and was supplying all I needed. It worked, I felt better.

On the first day of class, I didn't think the kids caught on that their teacher was more scared than they were. Only a couple of kids cried when their mother left and were fine shortly after. They called me "teacher," even though I introduced myself as Miss Louise. It made me feel good, so I let them. Plus, I thought it might also help me grow into the role. The morning moved along reasonably well; everything got done and on schedule, even though a couple of boys seemed to have their own agenda. The hardest part for me was the Bible verse. Not only did I need to remember the verse and try to sing it to the song tune, but I also had to remember all the hand motions that illustrated the words. It was a fun way for the kids to learn the verses, but I was really uncomfortable having to sing. The other teachers seemed to have an easier time with them and even enjoyed it. Not me; I struggled with it until something happened on the playground that changed how I viewed it.

While on the playground, I told one of the ladies who helped in my classroom about my hard time singing the verses. I confessed that as a child, I didn't learn any of the songs that are so familiar to most Christians. That's when I felt God say to me, "This is your gift, to give you what you missed in your childhood." It was so powerful I stood in awe, almost crying in front of the woman. Mumbling, I tried to tell her what had just happened, but I didn't think she understood. How could she? I didn't! The thought that I could be given an experience fifty-three years later that I missed as a child was so amazing. Who could do such a thing but God? And that He had done it for me was almost too much to handle.

Learning that this teaching position was a gift for

me changed how I looked at it. I tried to see it from the kids' point of view. Instead of worrying if I had what it took, I started to have fun with it. I also began to take advantage of the times the assistant children's director and other teachers came into my class to sing with the children. At those times, I decided to sit with the children and sing with them as if I were one of them. The kids seemed to like it. They sat close to me; one even climbed into my lap. It made me feel accepted, and I began to relax.

It wasn't long before I needed to be reminded of what God had said to me earlier. At the next leaders' meeting, I got a hug and encouraging words from the acting teaching director. She told me to relax and have fun. When I replied, "I just want to do a good job for God," I felt the Lord say, "You are still looking at it like a job. I told you it was a gift." "What do you do with a gift?" He asked. It seemed an easy question to answer, "Enjoy it, of course!" Still, I wasn't sure how being a kid would help me be a teacher, but I decided to trust God to work it all out. And in the meantime, I'd have fun!

When I said I wanted to see what my faith could do, I never expected it would be in a place like Teacherville. It was a foreign land to me. As much faith as it took for me to go there, it seemed to take an even greater faith to stay. I wanted to trust God, accomplish my purpose there, and enjoy the gift I'd been given. Yet, I was still wondering what I had to offer. God had kept His promise to be there and supplied my needs in amazing and unusual ways. The only doubts were about my own abilities. The struggle with my insecurities continued until I learned the root cause and discovered a certain power in a place I never would have considered.

10 COMMITMENTVILLE

The road leading through Teacherville had gotten rough. With one boy challenging even the most experienced sent to help in my classroom, it was becoming obvious that I was over my head when it came to disciplining children. Each week, I went home asking what I was doing there and not wanting to go back. I'd come to the point where I was ready to cash in the "Escape Clause" I'd been given before I agreed to go there when a sudden detour took me through Commitmentville and showed me a power I'd never known.

A strong sense of obligation to do what I say I'll do has always made commitment hard for me. I'd been careful to be sure I could do something before committing myself, which may be why I didn't get married until I was forty-one years old. Deciding to go to Teacherville was different. The only thing that qualified me to be a children's Bible teacher was my faith that God had called me there and had promised to be there with me. In my mind, it was a test of that faith. As much as I wanted to trust God, when it came down to it, my final decision had come after the teaching director at the time said, "Why don't you get started, and if you don't like it, come tell me, and we'll find you something else." I called it my Escape Clause.

Despite all the training, support from the other teachers, and God, I would have cashed in the Escape Clause weeks earlier. However, I wasn't sure if the new teaching director would honor it. The children's director and other more experienced teachers used the "time-out" method to discipline the boy but were unsuccessful. I'd been so caught up in seeking great faith that I'd forgotten that much of my journey so far had been learning about love. I decided to apply what I'd learned and see if it would make a difference in my classroom.

First, I announced to my class that I loved them. Then, one morning, an idea came to me while reciting the pledge of allegiance. The children in this Bible study organization were referred to as "Lambs," with each age group assigned a different color. My class, the four-year-olds, were "Blue Lambs." Hoping to unite our class, I'd often say, "We are all Blue Lambs, and we love each other." When one kid hit another kid, I would say, "We don't hit each other; we love each other." I also implemented what I called "Snack Chat." During the break, while the kids were eating their snacks, I asked if there was anything they wanted to talk about. To my surprise, I started to see the kids as "little people" and really began to love them. I also looked for opportunities to make friends with the boy who seemed to be causing most of the trouble. While on the playground, I'd spend a few minutes chatting with him. I complimented his apparent natural leadership abilities and invited him to help me in class, hoping he'd work with me instead of distracting the others. He agreed, but after the first couple of assignments, he returned to doing his own thing and encouraging others to follow him.

My plan to gain control of my class with love hadn't worked out; nothing had. Upset, I'd gone home, not wanting to go back. As I lay on my couch, I cried out to God, "I don't know what I'm doing there! I can't go there anymore! I'm going to talk to the teaching director and see if she will honor the Escape Clause." That's when I heard the preacher on the TV show I'd been watching say something I thought for sure was meant just for me. What I heard was: "God wants you to know He hears your cries. Your breakthrough is near, so don't quit."

The test of my faith finally came when I realized it wasn't the teaching director I had committed to. She wasn't the one who had led me to believe God wanted me to be there. And as much as the children's director wanted me to stay, she wasn't the one telling me not to quit. So, the real question was: "Could I quit on God?" I knew there was no way I could return to a life without God, so the only thing to do was keep going.

Once quitting was no longer an option, there was a power that came with being fully committed. I decided to give what I had to give and let God supply the rest. And that's when things began to change. Then, that boy's mother dropped out of Bible study, along with her son. It got easier after that, but at the same time, I felt like I'd failed him. And so, I continued to pray for him. I began to focus on the storytelling, using my graphic design skills to illustrate the Bible stories. I soon discovered that creating an interesting story for children to understand is not unlike simplifying an advertising message and adding visual effects. I started creating the lessons as I would like to have them taught to me. It was so much fun dressing up as one of the characters in the story and seeing the kids' reactions when their teacher looked like someone different each week. My favorite was when I suddenly appeared as an angel and announced that God was coming to earth as a baby!

On the last day of class, the mothers were picking up their children, and the kids were saying goodbye to each other. As he was leaving, one boy yelled to another, "I love you!" And the boy yelled back, "I love you too!" As his mother and I looked at each other surprised, I felt the Lord say in my heart, "That's what you're doing here."

After seeing how much easier, more fun, and successful things went when I was fully committed, I began to notice how much of the time my mind was divided between doing something and wishing I was doing something else. It was like a battle was going on in my mind, even over simple everyday tasks. I decided to bring the power of being fully committed to everything in my life. Whenever I found myself doing something and thinking I should be doing something else, I started telling myself, "This is what I'm doing right now!" It was amazing how much faster and more enjoyable even laundry became, leaving time for something else more fun.

I'd seen God's enabling power at work in my life to accomplish what I never thought I could do—teach children to love one another. I'd experienced what it's like to work with God, and I liked it. My faith had been tested, and because of it, I'd come to a greater determination to follow God wherever He leads me—no turning back. What's next, Lord?

11 HONORVILLE

The thought that God would honor me had never crossed my mind. Why would it? I thought it was all about honoring God. Adventures in Honorville not only took me to a deeper place of honoring God but to my surprise, my eyes were opened to see how God also honors me.

The time had come to decide if I would teach a second year in the children's ministry at Bible study. Sheets were passed out in the leaders' meeting, asking us to pray about it, check the yes or no box, and return our sheet the following week. So, I prayed, "Lord, should I teach another year, or are we moving on to something else?" I received an answer right away, but it didn't sound like something God would say. With all the divine guidance it had taken to get me to go to Teacherville and to stay when things got difficult, now He says, "It's your call"? It didn't make sense. *That can't be God,* I thought. So, I prayed again and again, but each time, I received the same answer.

When I didn't turn in my sheet the next week, the teaching director came and asked me if I was going to teach the following year. I told her I received an answer when I prayed, but I didn't think it was from God, so I was still praying about it. She asked me to tell her what the answer was that I received. After I told her, I asked her if she thought it sounded like something God would say. Immediately she said, "Yes, that's God honoring you!" "What?!" I blurted out, "How could that be?" She said God was leaving it up to me to choose. Either yes or no would be fine.

As much as I trusted the teaching director's knowledge of God and her faith, I had trouble with the idea that God would honor me. I had accepted that God loved me, but that He would honor me seemed too much for me to accept for some reason. Yet, it was the only answer I seemed to be getting. So, I took what the teaching director said as confirmation and asked myself, "What do I want to do?" Do I want to volunteer for another year in the children's ministry? It was a tough decision. I wasn't sure what I wanted to do. I loved being in the leaders' group and learning from and serving with the women of faith there. But could I endure another challenging year with the children? Learning and working with God was an amazing experience, and I couldn't help thinking there were more lessons for me there. Or should I move on to different lessons somewhere else? Was God telling me there would be lessons to grow my faith if I decided to stay or if I chose to go? Lessons did seem to show up wherever I was. So, as long as He was leaving it up to me, I decided I wanted to spend another year with the ladies I'd grown so fond of.

A lesson in honoring God came one Sunday, during a local radio program Jim and I frequently listened to on the way to church. *Back To The Beatles* with Jim Carson on KRTH 101 shared history and played old interviews from the early Beatles days. This particular Sunday, an interview with Paul McCartney was played. He told about having a bachelor pad where people would drop by and hang out. One day, a guy came to the front gate and said he was Jesus Christ. Paul thought he probably wasn't, but he didn't want to turn him away if he was. So, he invited him in, gave him a cup of tea, and chatted with him until it was time to meet the guys for a session. He told Jesus he could come along if he promised to sit quietly in the corner and not say anything. He said Jesus did come to the session and did sit very quietly. After that, Paul said he never saw the guy again. Jim and I both enjoyed the story and thought it was very interesting, especially considering we were on our way to church.

When we got to church, the sermon was on Creation. As often as I'd read and heard about the world's creation, I was given a new way of looking at it when the pastor stressed that God created everything from nothing. My mind wandered at that point to compare how I create something. I usually look to see what I have, then go to Home Depot or the craft store to get whatever else is needed. But the Bible says in the beginning, "the earth was formless and empty," which means God created everything from absolutely nothing!

On the way home, I was still thinking about it all. For some reason, hearing the creation story in that way made me more fully realize just how much more capable God is than anyone else. Then my mind went back to the Paul McCartney interview and the story of him having who he thought could possibly be Jesus right there in the room with him yet telling him to sit in the corner and not say anything. As I laughed at Paul for not consulting with the Creator of the universe when he had the chance, it suddenly occurred to me that I have Jesus inside of me and do the same thing all the time! I'm carrying around the One who created everything, the most intelligent Being on the planet, and how often have I ignored Him, I wondered.

So, what was the lesson in Honorville? Was it to wake me to the value and worth of who I have inside me—the One to whom all things are possible? Could it be with all I'd learned about trusting and following God, I'd grown worthy of God trusting me? What it all meant and where it was leading me, I wasn't quite sure. It was new territory. What I was sure of was that I was with the One who created this territory and was eager to see what He had to show me. I'm with You, Lord!

12 FAITHVILLE

My faith in God had grown to the point of believing anything was possible. Following the teaching of Jesus had brought me to the better life I'd hoped for, but something He said had me suspecting there was an even greater life to be found. Jesus said, "Anyone who believes in me will do the same works I have done, and even greater works." The possibilities of that excited me, knowing the works of Jesus included healing people, some of whom had already died! I was also highly intrigued by what the greater works could be. In Faithville, a brave attempt to share my faith with a dying friend turned out to be my first step toward doing the works of Jesus.

I'd been reading the book *All About Jesus,* compiled by Roger Quy. The book combines the accounts from the four gospel writers, Matthew, Mark, Luke, and John, so they can be read straight through as one continuous story. Having all the details of each story together in one place made it easier for me to grasp the amazing things that happened without having to continually look up the accompanying story. The book was also written in an easy-to-understand interpretation with a reference chart in the back that showed where to find the same stories in the Bible if I wanted to compare.

I liked the book so much that I bravely decided to share it with my next-door neighbor. Frances had spent several weeks in the hospital with complications from surgery. Jim and I visited her as she moved from hospital to rehabilitation, convalescent home, and finally to hospice. All we heard from her was how much she wanted to walk. She'd been through physical therapy and tried to keep her legs strong, but she'd been in bed so long that her muscles had begun to atrophy, and was told therapy would no longer help. That's when I got the idea to bring her the *All About Jesus* book, thinking it would give her something to do and might actually help build her faith for a miracle.

Even though Frances was a big fan of my blog, I wasn't sure she'd be interested in the books I was reading. When I gave her the book, she said she couldn't read it because she hadn't brought her glasses with her. I didn't say anything but wondered how she'd gotten along without them for so long. Thinking it was her way of saying no, I decided not to pursue the idea. She then surprised me and asked if I would read it to her. I was delighted. She noticed the marker I'd placed in the book and asked me to begin there. Thinking it would interest her, I had marked the story about the four guys who brought their paralyzed friend to Jesus to be healed. The house was so crowded where Jesus was that they couldn't get in. They ended up cutting a hole in the roof and lowered their friend down right in front of Jesus. After I finished reading the story, she said she liked it and believed anything was possible. Taking another brave step, I asked if I could pray for her. When she agreed, I laid my hands on her legs and said, "Jesus, Frances wants to walk and believes You can help her. So, I bring my friend to You to be healed so she can walk."

After I prayed, Frances wanted me to read some more. So, I read the story about the paralyzed man who had been at the pool for 38 years, waiting for someone to help him into the water at the right time. It's interesting how often I've read the Bible and noticed something I hadn't before. And this was one of those times. In other stories, Jesus spoke about the person's faith and said their faith had healed them. But in this story, Jesus only said to the man, "Pick up your mat and walk," and the man did! The man later got into trouble with the religious leaders for carrying his mat on the Sabbath. When asked who had told him to pick up his mat and walk, the man didn't know. Amazingly, the guy didn't even know who Jesus was and was healed!

Doubt started to set in with Frances. She didn't think she would be healed because "You're not Jesus," she told me. "Yeah, but in my prayer, I brought you to Jesus just like the guys in the story brought their friend to Him." She agreed but then told me I didn't pray right. She was so funny! She also said the stories in my book weren't true. That's when I told her they were right out of the Bible and showed her the reference chart, which listed where to find the same stories in the Bible. She then said something that really surprised me. She said, "Next time, bring your Bible so we can read both and compare."

During the next couple of visits, I read to her from my Bible the same stories I had read when I laid my hands on her legs and prayed for her to walk. I wasn't sure if she believed she would walk or if she just liked the fact that I was visiting her. That question was answered the morning Jim came home from next door and said that Frances' daughter was there taking care of things. When he asked about Frances, she said she had caused a big commotion, screaming for someone to come and help her walk. The nurses tried to calm her by explaining why she couldn't walk, but Frances got even more upset and kept insisting she could walk if someone would help her up. The daughter said they had to sedate her to calm her down. I felt so bad when Jim told me, thinking I'd caused it all. Once I thought about it, I saw all the commotion as an expression of her faith! Frances believed! I also believe she would have walked if someone had helped her. It must have been scary for her daughter, and I felt bad about that for a long time, but I was happy to know that Frances believed. Frances may not have been able to walk during the short time left on this earth, but I know she's now walking on the streets of heaven!

Later, I saw that the man in the Bible, the one by the pool of water, also demonstrated faith when he did what Jesus told him to do—he picked up his mat and walked. It made me wonder why I didn't help Frances to walk after I prayed for her. Or perhaps commanded her to get up and walk as Jesus did. Was it because I was afraid she wouldn't be able to? Could it be that I didn't really believe like I thought I did? As much as I thought

I'd grown, my journey through Faithville showed me there was still much to learn about the works of Jesus.

13 RESTVILLE

I'd been learning about God's finished rest, where everything needed has already been provided. I'd heard it's not an easy place to get to, but it's where you want to be for the best life possible or for the greater life, which I was hoping to find. My experiences in Restville confirmed much of what I had heard.

Getting ready to go on vacation has always been stressful for some reason. This time was even more so because I needed to see that my mother would be cared for while we were away. Though she'd become quite dependent on me for her survival, she still lived in her home as she had always wanted. As dementia slowly rendered her unable to remember how to do things she'd done all her life, I began doing them for her. Two or three times a week, I'd go over to do chores around the house, drive her where she needed to go, and prepare her meals. I'd put meals on plates in the refrigerator, ready to warm up in the microwave, which she could do. Other days, I'd call to check on how she was doing.

When the time came for me and Jim to plan our annual vacation, I struggled with whether to go. Calling my mom every day while we were away wouldn't be a problem, but who would prepare the meals and do what she needed around the house for seven days? The more I stressed over the decision, the more I felt the Lord encouraging me to leave it all up to Him. But how? It felt so irresponsible to go off and leave my mother with no one but God to take care of her. Finally, in frustration, I told God, "I can't just go off and leave my mother to starve!" That's when I felt the Lord say something that spoke volumes of where my faith was at the time. "Do you really think I'd let your mother starve?" He said. It left me stunned, not knowing what to say. This is the same God that dropped manna from heaven and quail from the sky to feed the Israelites in the desert. Even though I knew the amazing things God did in the Bible, it was still hard for me to imagine how He'd physically take care of my mother's needs in this day and age. Although I couldn't understand how it would actually happen, I decided to trust God and see how He'd work it all out.

The next time I was at my mother's house, her neighbor dropped in for a visit. When I mentioned our plans for a vacation, she insisted I allow her to check on my mom while we were away. One of my friends insisted on the same thing. I also received information about a caregiver service that had a one-hour minimum. Other times when I'd checked into in-home care services, they all seemed to have a four-hour minimum, which my mother wasn't comfortable with. She did agree to a two-hour stay, which I thought would work out great for the meals and chores. Before I knew it, all the help my mother would need was lined up, and Jim and I were able to get away, rest, and have some fun without worrying about my mom.

When we returned from Restville, I was reminded of another commitment God had encouraged me to start back in Commitmentville. We'd been attending our church for fourteen years and hadn't officially joined. Though we were active in the church, learning, growing, and serving, I never could see any added benefit of being a member over what we already had. When I questioned the Lord, He said it was the difference between living together and being married. From that, I understood that commitment helps you stay through the tough times.

Our church had gone through some tough times, as many had during the recession. The staff had been reduced to the bare minimum, and many in the congregation had left because of it. And after the senior pastor was asked to leave, many others left hurt and angry. It was hard seeing the church where I'd come to know God being dismantled and my friends leaving. Despite all the sadness and uncertainty, something I'd heard in one of the meetings had me excited and wanting to stay. It was the reason the elder board gave for letting the pastor go. They said they didn't want to, that it was really hard, but they couldn't go against what they knew was the Holy Spirit leading them to do. That's when I got excited. I thought if God was the one making the changes in our church, then something really good was coming!

The search for a new lead pastor had reached the point in the process for the congregation to meet the final candidate. No one said anything about having to be a member to attend the meetings, so Jim and I did. That's when my lessons from Commitmentville came into play. At the time, the candidate was pastoring a church in another state, so we met him electronically via FaceTime on the big screens. To let us know how serious he was about leaving his church, friends, and even some family behind, he told us he was "all in" if we decided we wanted him as our pastor. That got me thinking, and on the way home, I said to Jim, "That pastor isn't even here yet, and he says he's all in. We've been here fourteen years. Can we say we are "all in?" After talking about it, we decided to go ahead and take the required steps to become members of our church. We'd received the paperwork but decided to put it off until after we got back from vacation.

After vacation, I began to have the same doubts I'd had all along. "What difference would it make to join?" again, I wondered. And again, strong encouragement came from God. Sunday at church, the pastor delivering the announcements said, "I don't know why I feel I should say this, but I need to say, 'I'm all in' for someone." As soon as he said it, I knew it was for me. God was telling me to follow through with our church membership. So, we did.

Just as I'd heard, God's rest was a struggle getting there. But I learned that when I commit to stop trying to figure everything out, it allows God's wisdom and power to work in my life. And that's when everything I need shows up instead of me having to hunt it all down. As simple as it may have seemed at the time,

Restville turned out to be the beginning of a new leg of my journey that would teach me more about God's finished rest, what makes it possible, and what keeps me from getting there.

14 GRACEVILLE

I wanted to see more of God's provision in my life, yet it still seemed so unreal not having to do anything other than rest. As the lessons from Restville continued, I would learn more about what has made divine provision a reality and what keeps me from receiving it. God has a way of explaining things through circumstances in my life that I can't seem to get from only studying the Bible. When lessons started indicating it was time to leave the law behind in order for me to receive all that's been provided, God literally laid it all out on the table, where it suddenly became clear.

Lessons on the difference between God's law and grace that began in Zacchaeusville now seemed to be showing up everywhere. And again, I was being encouraged to leave the law behind and to continue on under grace. But how do I live without the law? And why would I want to? I didn't understand. The journey to understanding began with a question in my Bible study lesson. It was a personal question that asked if there was a sin I needed to confess. Nothing immediately came to mind, but after some thought, I did think of something I wasn't being completely honest about. Although I'd committed to caring for my mother, secretly, I didn't want to.

As good as it felt to finally admit it, I didn't expect anything more. But the next morning, I woke up with a scripture verse on my mind—"My grace is sufficient for you"—and just knew it was God's answer to what I had confessed. Not only was I inspired by getting the same answer the apostle Paul was given, but I also took it as confirmation that God wanted me to care for my mother rather than any of the other more popular alternatives. It should have been enough to overcome any obstacle, but by the next week, as I was running out of easy meal ideas to leave my mom, I found myself asking, "Lord, where is this grace, and how does it work exactly?" And so, my lessons on grace began.

While trying my best to care for my mother, each week, I was learning that nothing is too hard for the Lord. I also learned that everything I need for life and godliness has been supplied through the death, burial, and resurrection of Jesus. More than forgiveness and the way to heaven, I learned it was actually an elaborate plan to give back to man, through Jesus' obedience, everything that was lost in the Garden of Eden. Yet, with all I'd learned about grace, I still didn't understand why I needed to leave the law behind.

All the lessons seemed to come together at the Bible study year-end potluck brunch. I had been absent when the food sign-up sheet went around, and by the time I returned, all the spots had been filled. My leader told me to just come and enjoy. I decided I would since, by grace, everything had already been provided, but as the time grew near, I started to feel like I didn't deserve to enjoy the brunch unless I brought something. That's when I saw so clearly that I was judging myself by what I do instead of what Jesus did for me and how it can keep me from receiving God's blessings in my life.

Realizing that I was allowing or rejecting blessings into my life by what I felt I deserved made me wonder what other provisions I had been denying myself. How many other times had I said "no" to a blessing because I felt I hadn't earned it? That's when I finally saw how continuing under the Old Testament law, where forgiveness and blessings were earned by keeping the law, was making it harder to accept what Jesus did for me. I finally understood that trying to earn what Jesus did for me, only keeps me struggling in my own limited abilities when my life could be so much more with God's grace at work instead. I don't want to miss out on anything God has for me, so I've decided to stop judging myself by the law and just accept God's wonderful gift . . . and enjoy.

I finally accepted that my mother could no longer stay by herself when I checked on her and saw that she hadn't eaten anything I'd left for her two days earlier. That's when I packed some of her things and took her home with me. Life got a lot harder with my mom living with us, yet I found myself doing things I had never been able to do before all the lessons on grace. Once I started trusting God with my mom and believing His grace was sufficient for whatever my needs were, I began to see how much more got done in my day and how much more easily. The times when life got hard, I took as a signal that I was trying to do things with my own strength instead of relying on God's grace. I don't know how God does some things, and sometimes it still seems too good to be true, but now I know it is true. Not because I'm good but because God is good, and He loves me.

Experiencing a deeper understanding of grace that

so unexpectedly came from a moment of honesty with God had me wanting more. Since everything I need is there, I decided to stay in Graceville to see what else God would show me about His incredible gift and how it works in my life. And it wasn't long before He went to work showing me a new way of looking at . . . myself.

15 IMAGE AVENUE

For as long as I can remember, talking to oneself has been widely accepted. Talking to an orange, however, would still be considered strange, to say the least. Though it was probably my own thoughts projected onto the orange, it turned out to be one of three conversations that would profoundly change how I see myself.

My mother wanted a boiled egg, toast, and an orange for breakfast every morning. One time, while slicing an orange, it seemed to talk to me. It said it was the same as it was created, that it was created to be an orange and was happy to be the way it was. As weird as it was that an orange would be talking, it seemed even weirder to be interested in what it was saying, but I was. It went on to tell me it has accepted that it's an orange, different from other fruits, and in some ways different from other oranges. It's a Valencia orange; many specifically choose a Valencia orange, and that makes it happy. It doesn't try to be something different. It's happy just being what it is.

As I listened, I couldn't help wondering if I knew myself, as well as the orange, knew itself. I've always tried to change myself, thinking if I was better, I'd have a better life. I tried different things, hoping to find the one thing I was good at. When I wasn't able to find that one thing, I tried changing myself into what I thought I needed to be in order to be what I was meant to be. The orange helped me realize I wasn't accepting myself as I was created. I had been so busy trying to be something I thought I should be that I'd been missing out on being who I was. I began to see that instead of looking for what needs to change, I should look for what makes me me. And so, my journey through Graceville continued on Image Avenue.

Although I may not have known who I was, I knew what I didn't want to be. Even though I'd committed to taking care of my mother, trusting it was what God had for me to do at that time, I started to feel as if I was losing myself. The happier my mother was to be taken care of, the harder it was not to think I was giving up my life just so she could sit and watch television. I had thought all the studying, learning, growing, and following God would eventually lead me to do something great. And endless cooking, cleaning, and laundry were not what I had in mind.

One morning, while putting on my makeup and talking to myself in the mirror, I told myself, "You have become something you never wanted to be—a housewife! And sometimes you feel like a slave." Trying to bring myself up, I thought about how the leaders at Bible study are thought of as servants. And so I said, "You're not a slave; you're a servant of God!" That made me feel better until later when I turned on the TV and heard something I felt was God correcting me. What I heard was, "You're not a servant of God. You're a son." Bursting into tears, I thought, *Wow, that's God's grace bringing me up so much farther than I could have ever thought!*

The third conversation came while talking to God after a class I'd taken at church on worship. I'd been motivated to learn more about worship while reading about the miracle release of the apostle Paul from prison while he was praising and worshiping God. It made me wonder just how a person gets to a place where they can sing and praise God amid nasty and unfair circumstances. Each time I tried it, it wasn't long before I found myself complaining and questioning God for the tough times. This time, though, I saw a connection between Paul's worship and the miracles that followed.

For some reason, I'd always thought the only way to worship God was by singing, which I didn't do very well. During the class at church, I learned there were other forms of worship. As an illustration of different ways to worship God, the pastor told a fishing story about how adding a weight onto the lure helps it get to where the fish are. The story helped me better understand the purpose of worship, but a question about the weight had come to my mind. I asked, "Am I supposed to put the weight on the line, or is that something I allow God to do?" The pastor answered my question simply by saying, "It's according to your relationship with God."

Later that day, the story and my question kept circling through my mind. I thought about all the times, as a young girl, I'd gone fishing with my father. Not only had I fished for trout in a stream, like the pastor talked about, but I'd also lake fished for bass and even deep sea fished for albacore. Although I knew different tackle was required to fish in a stream than in the ocean, I wasn't sure what was needed where. I knew

I had my answer when I heard myself say, "My father knew, and he always prepared my line for me." God knows what's needed, so I'll allow Him to put the weight on! And so I asked, "Lord, how can I worship You?" The answer I received was profound, definitely not something I would have thought. What the Lord said to me was, "You can worship Me by thinking of yourself as I created you—in My image."

The Bible states that God made man in His image, but until this point in my journey, I hadn't taken it seriously. Mainly because God is God, and I didn't think I was anything like Him. After hearing it directly from God, it suddenly became very serious. The Proverb "As a man thinks in his heart, so is he," came to my mind as the way of getting there. Instead of striving to be like Him, as I had been doing, I needed to think of myself as already made in God's image.

Details and aspects of God similar to mine began showing up in Bible study, church sermons, and even through friends complimenting my character. I was surprised by how many references to the physical attributes of God I began to notice in the Bible. I also learned that God has thoughts and emotions. Along with powerful spiritual qualities given at my rebirth in Christ, they all pointed out to me ways I was already like Him. It left me feeling closer to God and wanting to learn even more about the likeness in which I'd been created. I specifically wanted to focus on Jesus, as the perfect image of God, to know more about what I'm capable of doing.

Until the realizations on Image Avenue, I'd been striving to be like Jesus, yet believing I couldn't actually be like Him this side of heaven. Being told by God to think of myself as He created me flushed out doubts I didn't know I had and told me that God cares how I think about myself. Thinking of myself as a daughter of God, created in His image, made a dramatic difference in how I cared for my mother. And to think God considers it worship when I do—that's amazing!

16 CANDY LANE

While the powerful lessons from Image Avenue continued to sink in and caring for my mother grew more challenging, I explored further into Graceville, hoping to find a fun escape. Over on Candy Lane, I discovered a computer game I liked to play and escaped there often. After noticing a spiritual principle while playing the game, it became even more interesting when it began to play out in my life. Unexpected twists and turns led me to a place I'd at other times elected to pass up. I also would have this time if not for the compelling purpose I was given for the hard lesson I was led there to learn.

Whenever I had a few extra minutes, I enjoyed playing Candy Crush Saga on my computer. The game was challenging and, at times, frustrating as I tried different strategies to get to the next level. Even with great strategy, most games ended in frustration without entry to the next level. Then, while playing one particular game level, I noticed that while I concentrated on the moves I could make at the bottom, explosions, and bombs were going off at the top that I had no thought or involvement in. Suddenly, I'd be at the next level with moves to spare, saying, "Wow! How did that happen?!" Stunned at how easily it all happened, it occurred to me—that's how it's supposed to work with God. When I do what I can do at the bottom, God does His thing at the top, and amazing things happen effortlessly without stress or frustration. As amazing as it was that a spiritual lesson would show up in a computer game, the lesson continued into my real life.

Though it had been long planned that a friend from Bible study would pick me up and we'd ride together to the children's teachers' Christmas brunch and gift exchange, in my mind, it was on Saturday, not Friday. Usually, I wouldn't answer the door in my nightgown, but that morning, I thought it may have been my next-door neighbor needing something. As I stood with my hair uncombed, wearing a sweatshirt over my flannel nightgown and fuzzy slippers, my friend smiled and asked if I was ready. It was so embarrassing! Wanting the whole thing to go away, I told her to go on to the party and I'd meet her there, but she insisted on waiting while I got dressed. My gift was wrapped and ready, but the dish I planned to take to the brunch was not yet prepared. "There's always plenty of food," she answered. Unable to talk her out of it, I invited her in and introduced her to my mother, who was eating her breakfast at the dining room table. While they chatted, I quickly went to get dressed.

Honestly, I probably wouldn't have gone to the brunch if my friend hadn't insisted on waiting. Showing up late without any food would have added to the embarrassment I was already feeling. As it turned out, I was glad I had swallowed my pride and went. Not only did I have a good time, but something happened that would make time for myself more possible. During dessert, the woman who takes care of the babies at Bible study came up to me and said, "If you ever want some time away from your mom, I'd be happy to stay with her." I was so surprised that an offer like that would come so unexpectedly. This was a woman I knew I could trust with my mom. A kind, loving woman, I felt confident my mom would like. And to think, if I hadn't gone to the brunch, I would have missed out on such an amazing offer. I couldn't help but think it was the

Candy Crush lesson showing up in my real life, but there was more to learn.

Things got even harder after coming home from my morning walk and finding my mother on the floor screaming in pain with a fractured hip. After a few days in the hospital and three weeks in a physical rehabilitation facility, she returned home needing help with things I really didn't like having to do. And the things I liked doing were even more difficult to fit in. That's when I began to suspect the lesson in caring for my mom was on humility. I was being humbled. I admitted to myself and God that I didn't like doing some of the things I had to do for my mother. And although I was trusting God and believing fun jobs were still to come, it was hard. At times, I wanted to quit but continued believing it was what God wanted me to do at that time, even though everything in me wanted to fight against it.

Then, one morning in the shower, while talking to God about my mom, I was given a purpose for the hard lesson on humility. Complaining, I said to the Lord, "She relies on me for just about everything, even things she can do for herself. It's like I'm her god." When I felt the Lord say, "You are," I said, "But I'm not a good God like You are. I don't love unconditionally like You do."

"Exactly," said the Lord. It made me sad to think how much she's missing by denying God. Knowing that God loves me has helped me so much, and now I'm starting to feel his power working in my life. So, I asked, "Lord, how can I help my mom know You?" That's when He said something that really got to me. "Through you," He said.

Candy Lane turned out to be quite different from the fun escape I expected. Realizing the things I was strategizing to do weren't nearly as important as the things I fought hard not to do caused a humbling effect on me. Finding out that my mother was experiencing God's love through what I did for her brought me to a new level in my journey. The lessons on humility, put on such a personal level, helped me to better understand its purpose. It's not about thinking less of myself and more of someone else like I once thought. It's about admitting that I don't know everything that God knows that allows God to do what I cannot. And what God wants is for everyone to know how much He loves them. It may have taken me a long time to get there, but humility was not as bad as I once thought. If by humbling myself, God can multiply my efforts, and from it, amazing things happen that I have no thought or involvement in—that's fun!

17 DRUM STREET

The humility lessons on Candy Lane had brought me to a new level of faith. Somehow, I knew there was still a way to go before I'd see the "greater works" that Jesus talked about. How much farther? I wasn't sure. While continuing through Graceville, events that seemed unrelated at the time came together on Drum Street to show me a picture of where I was headed.

I had hoped to finish my second year as a children's Bible teacher, but caring for my mom took so much of my time that I decided it would be my last year. Planning and acting out Bible stories for the children each week had been an amazing experience. I had followed God into unknown territory, and my faith had grown dramatically. My mom was also learning about God by watching me practice my storytelling and helping me prepare the crafts. As the end of the year grew closer, I began to cherish the moments that were left. Then, one morning, God assured me that my journey with Him would continue by reminding me that lessons can pop up anywhere.

It happened in the elevator on the way to my classroom. A woman who worked in the office of the church where the Bible study was held, had gotten into the elevator with me. As I stood with my cart piled high with all the supplies I needed to teach the children's lesson for the morning, the woman said, "That's a lot of coffee." Quickly, my mind searched for what she could be referring to, and still, I had no idea. Finally, I said, "What?" She then pointed to the giant clear bag of coffee containers at the very top of my cart. "Oh, that's not coffee," I told her, "Those are drums for the children to play; I'd forgotten they were coffee cans." That's when I felt the Lord say something to me. He said, "That's total belief when you don't remember what you used to be and only see what you are now." Wow! Immediately, I knew it was something significant, but then the elevator doors opened, and I went on to my class. Later, it was written in my journal and filed away in my mind with everything else I'd learned.

Giving up the children's ministry also meant having to leave the leaders' study group. Although I planned to return to the regular group study the following year, I would miss being part of the leaders' group where I'd learned so much being among believers mature in their faith. A surprise was coming for me, though; that would more than make up for what I would miss.

I got a call from the teaching director who initially called me to be a Bible study children's teacher. She had recovered from the life-threatening illness that had kept her from returning to Bible study and was working on creating a leadership manual for an upcoming class at her church. She asked if I would help her with the graphics for the manual. I was thrilled! Before she became sick, we planned to work together to add graphics to her Bible study lectures. I was disappointed and, at times, felt cheated out of something when she wasn't able to return. And so, I was excited to have another chance to work with her.

We started by meeting for breakfast to discuss her vision for the manual, which became weekly as the manual progressed. Discussions over the manual turned into lengthy personal conversations about God and what He was doing in our lives. Our conversations were so inspiring we didn't want them to end and would spend two to three hours talking. When the manual was finished and I was able to attend her class, it was like being back in Bible study with her again, only better. Our breakfast meetings continued monthly and turned into a treasured friendship. Each meeting was a bonus blessing as I listened and learned from her long life as a Christian and Bible teacher. And it's amazing to me that she says she learns from me too, when I share what God has been teaching me. Her special friendship and the encouragement she's given me for my book and blogs have meant so much more to me than whatever I thought I had missed out on at Bible study. Thank You, Lord!

When I wouldn't accept any payment for the work I'd done on the manual, she surprised me with a gift card to a local restaurant. I didn't know how to refuse such a gesture, so I politely accepted, not knowing how much of a blessing it would soon become. A couple of weeks before Thanksgiving, I fainted at the gym and broke my right arm. In some ways, things got harder afterward, and in other ways—more interesting. My mother stepped up and started helping me. She tied my shoes, like when I was little. She helped me cut up vegetables for dinner and with other things I had trouble doing with only one arm. When it came time for Thanksgiving, it turned out that the gift card my friend had given me was enough for a delicious "heat and eat" Thanksgiving dinner for our family.

Though I was grateful my arm healed without surgery and with minimal physical therapy, I was left with questions. When I first started to feel faint, I prayed for strength. So, why did I still faint? An answer came while watching a TV sermon on believing God's word over even your own body. It seemed pretty radical at first, but the more I thought about it, the more fascinated I became with the idea. Was that my answer? Did I follow my body instead of waiting for God's strength? Was I led by my pride to try and make it to the bathroom when I began to feel nauseous? I hadn't made it very far when I looked up and saw a crowd of people around me, all very relieved to see me waking up. It took some convincing, but I agreed to be taken to the hospital in an ambulance. Tests showed no explanation for fainting other than I shouldn't have tried to get my work-out in before lunch. I learned not to do that again, and my other questions were put away in the back of my mind.

The picture of total belief I'd seen on Drum Street seemed only to show me I wasn't there yet. How could I be with so many questions and doubts? The difference was that now stored away in my memory with all the questions was that picture of perfect faith I'd been given. It was that picture that would soon bring to my mind one question that would flush out all my other questions and send me on a year-long journey in search of an answer that would put my doubts about God to rest. I'll tell you about that next.

18 TREE CIRCLE

So, what was the question that sent me on a year-long journey in search of the answer? It came at church while listening to a sermon on the Garden of Eden. While thinking I'd heard it all before, the question suddenly popped into my mind, and the curiosity-led pursuit was on!

The question that came to my mind that Sunday morning was: What if God did not create the tree of the knowledge of good and evil? "What? That's absurd!" was my first reaction. *Of course, God created it; He created everything.* But before I could even finish that thought, my mind went to the parable Jesus told about the wheat and tares. On the way home from church, my mind raced back and forth, thinking it couldn't be true—but what if it was? I'd heard various explanations for why God planted the tree but had never heard anyone question "if" He planted it.

When I got home, I immediately went to my Bible. In the second chapter of Genesis, I read that God made every tree grow that was ... good for food. Then, in verse seventeen, God told Adam if he ate from the tree of the knowledge of good and evil, he would surely die. So, I determined that the tree couldn't be good for food. Could that mean God didn't plant it, and it somehow came later? But how? Then I found the parable of the wheat and tares in Matthew's gospel, which seemed to be the answer—the enemy planted it during the night. Still, it all just seemed too crazy. That's when I decided to email my pastor with the whole thing and let him straighten it all out for me.

My pastor thought they were all good questions and was glad to hear I was wrestling with the text. He also said he'd not heard anything other than that God had created everything in the Garden, nor anyone connecting the parable of the wheat and tares to creation. Still, I couldn't let it go. I had to find out why that question had come to me.

I couldn't help wondering why God would plant a poisonous tree in His perfect, peaceful Garden. Was it to test Adam and Eve's obedience, as I'd heard Christians say? I've never liked the thought of God putting His children in harm's way just to see if they would obey Him. It didn't sound like the loving, caring, encouraging God I had come to know thus far on my journey. The idea that the serpent planted the tree and then deceived Eve into eating the fruit made more sense. But how? Perhaps the serpent crossed what was already there like scientists do today? Then, when God noticed the hybrid in His Garden, He was warning Adam, not testing his obedience? But why didn't God just remove the tree? Jesus demonstrated how easy it would have been when He said to the fig tree, "No one eat of you ever again," and by the next day, it was dried up from the roots. The answer Jesus gave the disciples in the parable was to let the tares grow with the wheat until harvest when they would be separated. But my pastor and Bible teacher friend told me that in the parable, Jesus was referring to people, not plants, which brought me back to the dreaded idea of it being a test.

It was all I could talk about as I continued to wrestle with the questions, and it drove my friends crazy. Exploring all the scenarios was initially interesting, but when no real answers came, it got frustrating. When I thought I'd exhausted even my Bible teacher friend, she came through with an answer I could finally accept. She thought it through, studied it out, and concluded it all came down to a choice. "It wasn't about the tree," she said, "that tree could have been like all the other trees in the Garden. It was what God said about that tree that made it different." Adam and Eve had a choice to believe what God said about it or what the serpent said about it. That was the answer that rang true for me! It's a choice! God created man with his own "will," and is free to choose to do what God says or to go his own way. Once that became clear in my mind, I began to see other things I'd read in the Bible differently.

Eve obviously believed the serpent who told her she would not surely die. I also saw why she chose to believe the serpent–he made her think the fruit would make her wise. Sadly, she hadn't realized that God had already given her wisdom regarding the tree when He said they would die if they ate of it. That's when I saw so clearly that wisdom comes from God, not creation. I also noticed something I hadn't before. In front of the verses that tell of them eating the fruit, there's the verse that says: "Therefore a man shall leave his father and mother and be joined to his wife, they shall become one flesh." Adam was commanded to stay with his wife! So, after Eve ate the fruit and handed it to Adam, what would he do? If he believed God about the tree, he had to have thought Eve would die. Would he refuse the fruit and live, or would he eat the fruit and die to be with his wife? That's a tough choice!

Though there's no way to prove my scenario of Adam's reason for eating from the tree, how beautiful to think he chose to die to be with his wife. It completely changed how I felt about him and revealed feelings of blame and resentment I didn't know I held toward him. After forgiving Adam and Eve for bringing evil into the world, I realized it was already there before they ate from the tree—as a serpent speaking contrary to God. I also realized that I have the same choice as Adam and Eve—to believe God or someone else.

All the questions that had me running in circles for so long eventually revealed doubts that kept me from fully trusting God. I came to suspect the real reason I'd come to Tree Circle was to resolve in my heart that it was not a test of obedience but a choice. Realizing that I have the same choice today—to believe what God says or believe someone else—put the responsibility on me. I could no longer blame Adam and Eve or God for what goes wrong in my life. It's all made me more determined than ever to believe what God says just because He said it. It's also made me want to read my Bible more!

While sorting out what was true, what wasn't, and what may have been a new revelation, my eyes opened to an entire section of the Bible that I wasn't quite sure I believed. I'll tell you about that next.

19 PAUL BOULEVARD

A better understanding of where Adam and Eve went wrong had me not wanting to make the same mistake they did and more determined than ever to believe God's word over anyone or anything. The problem was that there was an entire section of the Bible I was afraid to accept. With lessons from Tree Circle still fresh in my mind, I came to Paul Boulevard, where I discovered a profound way of sorting out what I believed.

Seeing so clearly that Adam and Eve's actions revealed who they believed made me take a closer look at my own beliefs. I believed God—because He's God. I also believed Jesus—so much that I'd tried to do what He said as hard as it was sometimes, but the apostle Paul—not so much, just because he wasn't God. It's embarrassing now to admit, but there was a time I wondered if he could be the big deceiver the Bible talks about, who in the end times will deceive even the elect. It sounds crazy, but since Paul wrote most of the New Testament, I couldn't think of anyone alive at that time in a better position to also deceive the elect in the end times. For whatever reason, I thought it was safer to stick with what Jesus taught and avoid what Paul had to say. When it was announced at Bible study that our next study would be on Paul's epistles, I was less than thrilled. But the Lord had been showing me that it wouldn't change my life unless I believed what I was learning. So, I agreed to go to Paul Boulevard, where I saw a compelling reason to believe in Paul's teaching about halfway through the study.

Week by week, as the study of Paul's letters progressed, something stood out to me: Paul's suffering. Paul kept saying the same stuff over and over. And over and over, he was beaten and thrown in prison for what he was saying. Still, he didn't stop. He just kept saying the same things. That's when my experience on Tree Circle came back around, and I began to relate to Paul in a way I could believe him.

When the question: "What if God did not create the tree of the knowledge of good and evil?" first popped into my mind, I thought it was a new revelation from

God. It had come much like other things God had spoken to me—as a thought in my mind. I felt I'd come to the point where I could distinguish my own ordinary thoughts from the ones through which God spoke to me. And the question about the tree was no ordinary thought! It was one I wouldn't have thought in a million years!

Learning that most of what Paul was so desperate to share was given to him by revelation, caught my attention. I found myself relating to how he must have felt when those he was so eager to share the message with didn't believe him. Those who I had told about the tree hadn't believed me either. I understood how hard it must have been for the people in Paul's day to accept information so contrary to what they were taught all their lives. I also saw the gravity of their choice to continue to believe that keeping the law would save them or to believe what Paul was saying—that a connection to God the Father comes through faith in Jesus Christ. The only thing I had trouble relating to was the abuse Paul was so willing to endure to continue sharing his message. It made me ask myself, "How much would I be willing to suffer to tell the world that God did not create the tree that caused the fall of mankind?"

Paul's revelations were confirmed in scripture by Old Testament prophets. All I had to go on was a parable Jesus told about wheat and tares. Some strange looks I'd gotten can no way compare with the reactions Paul received. Still, it showed me just how much Paul must have believed the words he was saying for him to continue sharing them, knowing when he did, that he would be beaten and imprisoned. I think it's what the prison guards saw too, that caused them to come to believe in Christ.

Although I still believe the question about the tree came to me from God, I'm not so sure it had come to reveal anything different about the tree. After all, it came as a "what if" question, not an actual statement of fact. If its purpose was to get me to think about what's true and what isn't, it more than fulfilled its purpose! Knowing I wouldn't be willing to suffer very much if at all, to say for sure that God did not create the tree of the knowledge of good and evil, told me that people aren't willing to suffer for what they don't believe, not even for what they aren't quite sure they believe to be true. That realization helped me to accept Paul's teaching. It also caused me to sort out what I do and don't believe. I just ask myself one simple question: "How much would I be willing to suffer for that?"

Once I decided to believe Paul's teaching, my eyes opened to learning more about what Jesus accomplished on the cross, His gospel of grace, and the powerful truth of who I am in Christ. I'm excited to see how my life will change.

20 TRUDY AVENUE

The last class in the series Jim and I had been taking at church was scheduled at a hotel on the beach about an hour away as a bit of a retreat. Looking forward to a little time away from caring for my mother, I elected the overnight stay option. I had lined up a caregiver to stay with my mom, but she was admitted to the hospital the week before the retreat. It was serious this time. Doctors and nurses had been instructing me about hospice and leading me that way. As a Christian, I wasn't sure if hospice was the right thing to do and was waiting on God's guidance, looking for the slightest indication as to what He would have me do. When it came, it came in a way that still blows me away when I think about it.

With all the difficult decisions, I needed time away from the pressure more than ever. Since my mom was being well cared for in the hospital, we decided to go ahead with our plans to attend the class retreat. I had also decided to focus on what we were learning and wouldn't talk about what was going on with my mother to anyone while we were there.

The morning of the class, I spotted two available seats next to a woman we had enjoyed discussions with previously. Also, a couple I hadn't met before was already seated at the table. They turned out to be retired missionaries from our church. When they started talking about the book they had written, *I Heard Their Cry,* I immediately thought our seating arrangement was no coincidence. I had just posted on my blog what was to be the final chapter of my first book, *A Different Way,* and had been researching publishing companies. I was even more surprised to hear their publishing company was one I'd talked to about my book. Now was my chance to learn more about the publisher and the entire process. But as it turned out, God had more pressing information for me to know from these missionaries.

After finishing the buffet-style lunch in our classroom, there was more than an hour left before class was to reconvene. When the missionary couple asked if we'd like to come along for a walk on the beach, I jumped at the chance to talk more with them.

Once we made our way to the beach, Jim and Ray paired up and walked ahead of Virginia and me. Virginia started our conversation by casually asking, "How was your week?" Still not wanting to talk about what had been going on with my mother, I said, "Oh, you don't want to know," hoping she would change the subject. Instead, she stopped and looked at me with genuine concern.

Then it all spilled out. The entire horrible story about my mom being in the hospital and because of her dementia, the doctors were looking to me for decisions on how far to go with treatment, and about them educating me on hospice care and how confused and undecided I was feeling. That's when Virginia confessed to me something so surreal. She said, "I'm a hospice nurse." Instantly, without saying anything, we both knew God had set us up. We stood there, crying, looking at each other in utter amazement.

Virginia, telling me she was a hospice nurse, clarified whether it was right for a Christian. Not only was she a Christian, but her lifelong service to God as a missionary also told me she was a strong, committed Christian. It couldn't have been more evident to me that my encounter with Virginia was the guidance I'd been looking for from God. But was hospice what my mother would choose if she could understand?

The fact that my mother was so willing to endure all the medical procedures without complaint still made the decision to move her to hospice care hard for me. I'd learned from home health nurses, who had previously come to the house, that even with dementia, they would not violate my mother's will. If she said "No," they would not continue. It was her choice. But this time, she hadn't said no to anything, making me think her will was to proceed with the life-saving treatments.

Soon after the retreat, there came the point where a particular procedure was necessary for my mom to live but would leave her in a condition where I knew she would not want to live. As hard as the decision was to discontinue all treatment and make her comfortable with hospice care, it was finally clear to me it was the right thing to do for her. It was time to let her go. She was in hospice for two days and then in heaven. But was she?

I hoped she was in heaven, but I wasn't sure. I never was able to get her to go to church with us. But with all the sermons I watched on Christian television, she had been exposed to God's word when she lived with us.

She had heard us read our Bible aloud and talk about God. She'd also willingly joined hands with us while we prayed at meals. But was it enough?

There was also the time I'd gotten frustrated with her saying, "I can't!" all the time, especially when it came to exercise. It got to the point where she needed a wheelchair around the house. The wheelchair didn't fit through the doorway to her bedroom, so she had to walk a few steps to her bed. One day, she caught on that I was having her get out of the chair a little further down the hall each time. When she refused to get up, saying, "I can't," I yelled, "Yes, you can! You can have the strength of Jesus!" Instead of getting mad and yelling back like usual, she looked at me so sweetly and, with a sincere voice, said, "I can?" I said, "All you have to do is ask Him. Do you want to ask Him right now?" She agreed, so together, we prayed and asked Jesus to give her His strength. Thinking about it later, after she passed, I asked God, "Was that enough for her, Lord? Did she make it with You to heaven?"

The answer came while reading my Bible in Acts 2:21: "Whoever calls on the name of the Lord, will be saved." I knew she had done that when she called on Jesus for His strength.

Interestingly, while making calls to inform family

and friends of my mom's passing, my physician cousin wanted to know the details of her death. After telling him the whole story, he said, "Wow, she had strength. A younger person couldn't have taken all of that."

Caring for my mom was quite a stretch for me, but with God's help, I went the whole way. And I'm glad I did; I have no regrets. All that could have been done to give my mom every chance to live was done without going too far, leaving her in a condition she wouldn't have wanted. Best of all, I'm at peace knowing she made it to heaven. Thank You so much, Lord!

21 SHEEP ROAD

I had heard God speak within me, and each time had been a profound experience. I'd also followed God to places way outside my comfort zone, learning to do things I would never have guessed I could do. On Sheep Road, I was led to believe that hearing God's voice and following Him can become more natural than I thought.

About half of the way home from visiting our Texas friends, we decided to stay the night in New Mexico. While pulling into a parking space in the motel lot, I heard a voice within me say, "Park on the other side." Quickly comparing the two spots, I thought, *Oh, what's the difference?* and continued into the first space, ignoring the little voice. Unfortunately, I discovered the difference between the two parking spaces while we were leaving.

As I was backing out of the parking space, there was a loud crashing noise, and our car suddenly stopped and wouldn't go any further. I had hit something, but what? I couldn't see anything. It turned out to be a concrete planter directly behind our car, too low to be seen in the rearview mirror. I probably could have seen it in the backup camera and heard the warning beeps if I'd been paying attention instead of talking to Jim at the time. Too late for any of that; the damage had been done. What bothered me the most was ignoring the little voice, especially after realizing that if I'd obeyed the voice, the planter would have been in front of the car, allowing plenty of room to safely back up.

It was a hard lesson, but it got my attention and motivated me never again to ignore the voice. Though I tried, there were still times when I wasn't sure if it was God's voice or just my own thoughts in my head I was hearing. Feeling unsure about when to follow the voice and when not to, the voice showed up to help me.

It happened at Bible study while serving as audio/visual tech—another job I'd been called to do that I knew nothing about. I planned to continue another year as a greeter, a role I'd become quite comfortable in since I was a greeter at my church. But when I reported to the door the first morning of the new class year, I was asked to serve as an audio/visual tech. "What?!" I replied, "I know nothing about that!" What could I say after learning that my name had come to the leaders' council while praying for God to provide someone for the position? I couldn't say no to God, so here I go again, learning something new.

I was shown to the sound booth and started by merely doing what I was asked to do. Later, there were a couple of training sessions to learn the equipment basics, but mostly, I learned by doing it each week. Along with setting up the microphones and equipment for the worship team, I was responsible for "mic" ing the teaching director before her lecture and removing it afterward. I also advanced the PowerPoint slides by following her cues. This one morning, her outline had several more points than usual, and she spoke quickly to fit them all in, so fast that the ladies had trouble filling in the answers on their printed outlines before the next slide appeared. A couple of ladies came to the booth during the lecture to inform us about it, and we told them we'd put the answers up at the conclusion.

At the conclusion, my routine was to make my way up the aisle to remove the teaching director's microphone, squeezing by all the ladies on their way out. That morning, they were blaming me for missing answers on their outlines. One lady even stopped me and said, "You can't go that fast. You need to slow down!" I quickly answered by saying, "I follow Sharon's cues." As I continued to the stage, these words came to me: "You knew who to follow in that instance. It can be the same with Me." Immediately, I knew it was the Lord. There was no doubt. I was so excited when I reached the teaching director that I blurted out what had happened and what I had heard the Lord say to me.

Not long after, I came upon an online sermon series based on what Jesus said about hearing His voice: "My sheep hear My voice, and they follow Me." Pastor Keith Moore talked about what it said in ways I hadn't thought before, pointing out that the only qualifier is being one of His sheep. I knew I was. I had accepted Jesus into my heart and was trying to follow Him; I just hadn't thought of it as the only requirement to hearing His voice. Also, seeing that it's a fact that His sheep hear His voice confirmed that it had been God's voice I'd been hearing throughout my journey. So then, if I'd already been hearing His voice, what was the Lord trying to tell me that morning at Bible study?

After some thought, it became apparent that I needed help with the "following" part of the verse since

I had heard His voice and still ended up wrecking our car's bumper. So, I did what Pastor Moore did and went line by line dissecting what God spoke to me. First, I heard Him say, "You knew who to follow in that instance." So, I asked myself, "How did I know to follow Sharon?" She's the teaching director; following her came with the decision to accept the tech position. She goes over her lecture notes each week, giving me cues, so when I hear her say certain things, I'll know what to do. That's when the second part, "It can be the same with Me," started to make sense. I can follow God the same way I knew to follow Sharon! It's the same process—following Jesus came with my decision to accept Him into my heart. He has given me a copy of His notes (the Bible) and has put His voice (the Holy Spirit) within me, so when I hear Him say certain things, I'll know what to do.

It finally dawned on me that the lesson on Sheep Road was on learning how to follow God's voice over all the other voices, including mine, that are clamoring for me to follow them. Seeing it so powerfully illustrated in my personal experience helped me to realize I've been given everything I need to follow Him; I only need to pay closer attention to what I see in the Bible and what I hear Him say within me.

22 LEGION HILL

While helping with the check-in desk at my cousin's church conference, I noticed a man sitting in the corner watching me. When the line caught up, and he made no move toward me, curiously, I said to him, "Can I help you?" His reply was even more curious: "The Lord has something I'm supposed to say to you, but I don't know what it is." What?! I said, "Are you sure it's for me?" Not only was he sure, but he further explained that the Lord had him stay every time he tried to get up and leave. At that point, we were both fascinated as to what the Lord was up to. Hoping the message would come to him, we chatted a little. I found out he was the pastor of the motorcycle ministry serving as security for the conference, which calmed my suspicions. At about that time, word came from inside the meeting for us to quiet down, so we ended our conversation.

Later that day, I had the chance to talk with the man again. The message still hadn't come to him, but he was interesting, and I felt there was much to learn from him. As I listened, he began talking about the man in the Bible with many demons called Legion. I knew the story well since it's where I got my purpose for writing my journey, but I'd never heard what happened to the pigs described that way before. When he said, "Those pigs couldn't stand the demons for even a few minutes, and they went and killed themselves," I just knew it was what the Lord wanted him to tell me. Although planning suicide was where my journey with God had begun, I hadn't ever connected suicide to that story before, but suddenly, there it was.

When I got home, I took a closer look at the story. Other times, my focus had been on Jesus telling Legion to go back and tell his friends what God had done for him, which is my purpose verse. This time, I noticed the various people in the crowd who asked Jesus to leave, the ones Legion was sent back to talk to. Some were the herdsmen who had witnessed their herd run over the cliff after Jesus cast the demons from Legion, and they entered the pigs. Many had heard what happened as the witnesses fled to the nearby towns.

And many more had heard from those who had heard it from the witnesses as the news quickly spread. When they all rushed out to see for themselves, they found Legion clothed and in his right mind, sitting with Jesus. The Bible says they were frightened and asked Jesus to leave. Legion wanted to go with Jesus at that point, but that's when Jesus told him to go back and tell his friends what God had done for him.

After getting a better look at the people Legion was sent to talk to, I was a little frightened too, and questioned the Lord regarding my purpose, "Lord, You want me to talk to people who are mad at You?" His answer to me was, "Keep reading." Then I saw the very last line at the end of the story that read, "and the people marveled." *How fun,* I thought, *I could handle that!* A few months later, the Lord revealed something from my childhood that would give me a more personal view of the story.

Soon after my book *A Different Way* was published, I was invited to share my testimony and talk about my book in front of a Sunday school class at our church. While practicing what I had prepared, I started with: "I wasn't raised knowing God. God was never spoken of in our home." The Lord interrupted me and said, "That's not true." What? I said, "Lord, how can that not be true? When were You ever spoken of in our home?" He answered, "Through the swear words." Stunned, not knowing what to think, I kept the revelation to myself for a long time.

Thinking back to my childhood, I remembered times of loud swearing, which included the words God and Jesus. I just hadn't considered that I was learning about God in that way. I wouldn't think it counted, but apparently, it did. I couldn't help but think hearing those words in anger, even though I didn't know what they meant at the time, may have kept me from knowing the love of God sooner in my life. I also wondered how many others had learned about God that way. It could be significant to share with others. Still, at the time, I wasn't comfortable revealing it about myself. Yet, it stayed on my mind.

My mind kept going back to Legion and the people who blamed Jesus for the loss of their pigs. I wondered if I'd been raised by someone who had held something against God. It would explain a few things. Another part of the story I'd usually overlooked because I didn't understand it was beginning to make sense. At the end of Mark 5:19, where Jesus tells Legion to go back and tell his friends what God had done for him is the phrase, "and how He has had compassion on you." It was the compassion Jesus had for Legion and his living conditions that moved Jesus to cast the demons from him despite the risk to the pigs. I also began to see Jesus' compassion for the townspeople even though they asked Him to leave. I saw it as His purpose for sending Legion back to talk to them—so they could also understand God's compassion for them.

It finally occurred to me that I could have been all of the people on Legion Hill at one time or another. I had first heard about Jesus through angry, fearful words. And I may not have directly asked Jesus to leave, but there were times I'd passed on opportunities to learn about Him. Though it came later in my life, I'm grateful for encountering Jesus to have my demons and doubts driven out through the lessons along this journey. I can relate to wanting to be with Jesus, yet hearing the call to go back and tell my friends what God has done for me. So glad, unlike Legion, I can have Jesus with me as I do. And for sure, I'm one who marvels. Now that I've learned compassion was God's purpose for sending Legion back to tell his story, my purpose has become clearer. By telling what God has done for me, I'm extending His compassion to others.

23 VISION DRIVE

I'm no longer feeling satisfied with having God help me in my ordinary life. I want to live the life of Christ that's now in me. I want faith to do the things Jesus did. I want to see the sick healed, blind eyes opened, and yes, even the dead raised. I believe Jesus still does those things. And I'm so curious to know what the "even greater things" are that He told the disciples they would do. I can't see how it will come about, but I know they are the desires of my heart.

On a Christian television program, I watched a woman describe her vision of the glory of God coming like a tsunami. In her mind, she saw people going into hospitals, laying hands on the sick, and these people, getting up and going home that same day. She saw a healing revival break out in hospitals, schools, churches, and at Wal-Mart. She believed there would come a time when you would hear "Healing line on aisle nine" announced over the loudspeaker. When she said that, I had a little vision of my own. I pictured myself at Wal-Mart, helping a man in a wheelchair who asked me to reach something for him on the top shelf. When I handed it to him, I asked him if I could pray for his healing. "Sure," he said. A lady who overheard me praying also wanted me to pray for her. So, I did. Then I heard it announced over the loudspeaker, "Healing line on aisle nine." When I looked up, a long line of people were waiting for me to pray for them. Wow, could that really happen? I wondered. I didn't know, but I was excited and curious.

I shared the vision with my Bible teacher friend at our next breakfast meeting. She told me she believed in divine healing and even shared a couple of times she had been healed. Then, she advised me to examine my motives for wanting to see people healed. It seemed obvious to me, but she explained that she had known some, and the Bible tells of those who acted from their egos, wanting prestige, the praise of men, and money.

It was a good question, so I did as my friend advised and asked myself, "Why do I want to heal people?" Besides helping people be healed and free from tortuous disease, the thought of the power of God coming through me was exciting. Could that be from my ego? The more I thought about it, the more I felt like I'd already learned that lesson. In the past, I had thought success would make me feel good about myself, but it only made me feel worse when I failed. It's been a journey, but learning how God thinks of me has made me feel good about myself in a real and lasting way. Nothing compares to knowing God loves me and is for me. Now, when I fail, I know it doesn't change that I'm a child of God. It just makes me want to learn how to do better next time, and who better to learn from than God, my Father? My motives now are to know God better and to learn how to accept everything He's given me to become who He's created me to be.

When I look around, I see so many sick people. While at a pharmacy waiting for a prescription to be filled, I noticed the entire back wall was shelves full of bags ready to be picked up. And that's only one pharmacy. How many pharmacies are there in my city, state, or country with walls like that one? I thought to myself, *that's a lot of sick people that Jesus has already healed by His death on the cross.*

Looking back over my journey, I felt I'd been led to want to help others receive what Jesus has provided for them, but trying to explain it to my friend got really confusing. So, to keep it straight in my mind, I drew a flow chart and then emailed it to her. (See chart below.)

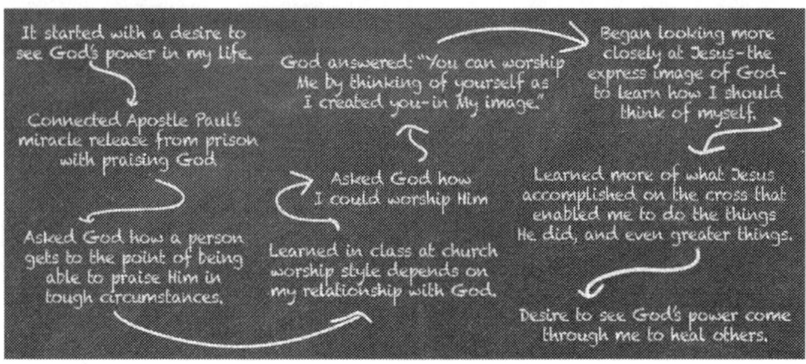

My friend said my chart made sense and that longing to serve Christ is the best motivation possible. She said she had known some who wanted to be seen or noticed, but that was not my motivation. She just wanted to make sure that I knew it. She also said there were very few healing ministers, which I had already noticed and wondered why. Very few seem even interested in God's healing these days. I bought a Bible study on divine healing with a video and study guide. I thought it would be fun to do a small group study and invite friends to learn together with Jim and me. So, I posted short descriptions of what we would be studying each week on Facebook and invited all interested in joining us. But no one came. So, Jim and I enjoyed the refreshments, watched the video, and asked each other the study questions. I was disappointed that no one showed up, but I kept posting the weekly study descriptions, hoping someone would come. Jim and I committed to finishing the study, group style, even though we were the only ones.

Then, one morning, I had a revelation about a vision I shared way back in Opportunityville. Most of my other lessons were about putting something or someone above God. Opportunityville had that too, when I had put bowling above God. But I started thinking about the person of great faith I had placed between God and me. That was new; I didn't remember ever putting anything between God and me. Wondering what that was all about, I thought about the vision I described in Opportunityville: my left foot stepping into the person of great faith and my right foot stepping into the leadership position. At the time, I thought I would become that person, and by doing so, it would bring me closer to God. But as I continued thinking, that's when the revelation came. I thought about how Jesus is the only person between God and me. And so that person of great faith—would be Jesus! The vision was me stepping into Christ, the author and finisher of my faith! And He is also my leader! Wow, what a vision!

Vision Drive gave me a lot to think about. I was excited about the amazing possibilities and, at the same time, struggled with thoughts of the kind of life I may be headed toward. With so much still to be learned about the healing Jesus provided on the cross and how to receive it, I have a feeling by the time I've learned and accepted who I am in Christ and have stepped into Him, I'll be ready for whatever comes with it.

24 TRUST TRAIL

My desire to see God's power come through me to heal others in my life greatly intensified when my husband was diagnosed with cancer. Fear could have easily derailed my pursuit of God's healing as we waded through complicated medical information so focused on what all the numbers meant in terms of treatment and life expectancy. But in those moments of fear, I recognized we weren't trusting God. Trust Trail took us through some rough territory but would eventually bring us together to a new level of faith.

One Sunday, a pastor at our church overheard Jim telling a friend about his diagnosis. The pastor later shared with us that he was a few months ahead on the same journey. He then invited us to his home, where he and his wife shared what they had been through and what we might expect. Talking with them made us feel that we weren't so alone. Each week at church, the pastor checked on our progress and answered any questions we were having. And when it came time for Jim's surgery, he organized a prayer session with the other pastors. After briefly sharing our needs, they formed a circle around us, laid hands on us, and prayed. I can't tell you how much that meant to us.

Something the pastor and his wife emphasized while talking with them stuck with me and changed my thinking. They stressed that the two of us were on a journey together, not just Jim. That thought had me going with Jim to all his doctor appointments, listening to image scan results, and discussing treatment options. It got even scarier when a spot appeared on one of the images taken to ensure the cancer hadn't spread. The report stated it was "likely cancer," but to be sure, a biopsy was ordered.

Since we were on this journey together, I started involving Jim more in what I was learning about God's promises for healing. We started reading scripture out loud to each other. We also began watching healing sermons and testimonies regularly on TV and online together. When we discovered that one of the pastors we watched on TV, also held a Sunday evening healing school service at his church not far from where we live, we decided to check it out. It turned out to be much like a regular church service, only the teaching focused on healing scriptures to build faith for healing. After that, whenever a pastor we watched on TV came to a town near us, we went to see them to learn what they had to teach us, and Jim never missed an opportunity for prayer.

We ventured out and gained greater exposure to the knowledge of God's healing power when my cousin, who pastors a small congregation in the Los Angeles area, invited us along on her speaking and healing prayer weekend at a private home a few hours away in Northern California. A doctor who had recently been healed of stage 4 liver cancer was inviting friends and family for prayer, hoping for the same outcome. My cousin planned to give my book as gifts and have me there to sign them; it would also be another opportunity for Jim to receive prayer. It was an extraordinary experience for us not only to see healing taught and ministered in that type of intimate setting but also for me as a new author. The people were all so friendly, and it was fun getting to know them as I signed their books. But most of all, I was hoping to see a miracle!

The biopsy turned out negative, thank God! The

doctors were confident the cancer had not spread. But with all the prayer, we expected the cancer to disappear. I was surprised, yet so proud of Jim when he boldly asked his doctor to rerun the blood test to see if anything had changed. Initially hesitant, his doctor followed Jim's wishes and reran the test. When the results hadn't changed, surgery was then scheduled.

The surgery was a success! We were told the cancer had been contained in the now-removed organ, leaving no signs it had traveled outside of it. We went home relieved and grateful. However, Jim's three-month post-op blood test showed that the cancer had aggressively returned. So again, we were back to image scans and consultants. This time, cancer was found in a part of the body that could quickly spread throughout the system.

While Jim's doctors were determining a course of treatment or if treatment was even an option, my cousin wanted me to do a book signing at her church. A guest healing pastor was scheduled for that particular Sunday, giving Jim another opportunity to receive prayer. After the teaching, Jim got in the prayer line, and I went to the foyer to sign books for those leaving. When Jim's turn for prayer came, the minister asked him to get his wife so he could pray for us both. His prayer turned out to be prophetic. He first talked to Jim and told him he was joyful and had faith, adding that we would live a long life and do something together. He then turned to me and said I was obviously a woman of God but needed some encouragement. He took my hand, put his other hand on my head, and said the Lord was healing the right side of my brain. He also said there was more to learn and that God would teach me. He said I would step into a new level of faith and leadership and would teach and testify. As much as the prophetic prayer boosted our faith for a future together, it wasn't long before I needed another dose of encouragement.

There was a lot on my mind as we sat in an examining room, waiting for the radiation oncologist to come in and tell us whether or not he could help us. I wanted to be strong for Jim, but at the same time, I was afraid. I thought about how the Lord had been teaching me to be like a little kid, to have fun, and to trust Him. Silently, I asked, "Lord, how would I be a little kid in this circumstance?" He quickly answered, "In this circumstance, your parents would be here with you." Suddenly, I felt the presence of the Father, the Son, and the Holy Spirit enter the little room. And before I could react, in came the doctor. He told us he had reviewed everything and was confident he could kill the cancer.

Trust Trail turned out to be a bumpy road. Through all the ups and downs, twists and turns, we learned that though our faith fails at times, God showed us He is faithful, and in that, we can trust.

25 PRACTICE COURT

If I wanted to begin seeing the supernatural things of God, I needed to start putting all that I'd learned from scripture, ministers, and prayer meetings into practice in my life. I figured if Jesus spoke out what He wanted to see, I needed to start doing that. I needed to pray for people out loud whenever and wherever the opportunity presented itself. So, that's what I started doing. And when I realized God was coaching me, the real learning began.

Opportunities abounded while greeting at church. I started to notice when I'd shake someone's hand and ask, "How are you doing?" they would tell me about some pain or condition they were having. As they passed, I quickly said, "Be well in Jesus' name." One morning, a lady told me she had lost one of her hearing aids. She had already combed through her house several times to no avail. She didn't know what she would do, explaining that it was costly to replace and she couldn't afford it. I reached for her hand and said, "Let's pray about it." She agreed, so I asked God to show her where to find the hearing aid. After praying, I told her to go about her day, and most likely, it would show up in a place she wouldn't have thought to look.

Later that day, the lady called me all excited. She said she found the hearing aid, and it was on a table she hadn't thought to look at, just as I had said! She couldn't wait to tell me about it and had searched through the church directory until she found my number. I was excited for her and motivated even more to pray for people, whatever their needs were.

Sometimes, I'd get all caught up in the person's symptoms, feeling sympathetic, and it wouldn't occur to me to pray for them. The Lord began pointing out these missed opportunities, like when Jim and I were at a party next door. We talked with our neighbor's sister and husband as they passed their two-week-old baby back and forth between them, trying to keep her from falling asleep. They said the baby slept when they were awake and was awake when they should be sleeping. "We're so sleep-deprived," they told us. They had been taking turns being up with the baby, thinking she might sleep through the night by keeping her awake, hopefully changing her sleep pattern. Then suddenly, they both got up and handed me the baby, saying, "Don't let her go to sleep," as they made their way to the dance floor.

As happy as I was to give them a little break, it didn't take long before the little one started falling asleep. I tried shifting the baby around on my lap to wake her, but it wasn't working. She looked so peaceful, I hated to wake her. The parents weren't happy, though, when they came back and found her sound asleep. On our short walk home, I was feeling bad for them. Then I felt the Lord say, "Why didn't you pray the baby would sleep through the night?" Good question! Why didn't I? I couldn't believe I had that baby in my arms and didn't think to pray for her!

More and more, as I heard people tell me of their health conditions, I'd ask them if I could lay my hands on them and pray for their healing. Most said yes and were grateful. Some said no, and I didn't push it. I also discovered that Christians have different beliefs about what the scriptures mean. When I told a woman, "And by His stripes, we were healed (Isaiah 53:5)," she said it didn't mean physical healing. She even laughed that I would think it did. That surprised me, knowing she'd been a Christian all her life. I began to wonder if I had it wrong.

Being laughed at challenged me to strengthen my faith for healing. I asked God if it were true that we weren't physically healed by His stripes. Had I misunderstood? I found in Matthew 8:17 that Jesus fulfilled the Isaiah 53:5 prophesy, saying, "He, Himself, took our infirmities and bore our sicknesses." That confirmed for me that physical healing was included. But Jesus continued healing all who were sick, blind, deaf, and dead, giving me the impression that it was ongoing. Later, He gave the disciples power and even commanded them to heal the sick, cleanse the lepers, raise the dead, and cast out demons. I couldn't see how that could be misunderstood, but the Lord had more for me to learn.

I had a revelation while watching a healing minister on TV. She was talking about how if Jesus said to do something, He also gave the ability to do it. She used Matthew 10:8 as proof, "Heal the sick, cleanse the lepers, raise the dead, cast out demons. Freely you have received, freely give." Her point was that since they had received the power for healing, they could then give healing to others. The revelation I saw was that believers in Christ have received healing and are commanded to give it to others. And I didn't need to convince anyone of it; I just needed to give others what I had been given. It's what the apostle Peter must have meant when he told the lame man begging at the temple gate, "Silver and gold I have not, but what I have I give to you: In the name of Jesus Christ of Nazareth, rise up and walk." Peter helped him up, and immediately, his feet and ankle bones received strength. The man went leaping into the temple, praising God. It gave me hope that I would see someone healed!

I prayed for the eyes of the woman who laughed at me to be opened, as mine were. A few weeks later, she complained about pain in her knee. Courageously, I put my hand on her knee and said: "In the name of Jesus, be healed." I was so surprised when she immediately said, "I claim that!" Afterward, the Lord asked me, "Why didn't you tell her, that her faith had healed her like I told people?" I thought it was the Lord's way of letting me know I'd missed an opportunity to confirm the woman's healing. Yet, the next time I saw her, the pain in her knee was all gone!

For a long time, I'd wanted to be in a Bible study group with those of great faith so I could learn from them. On Practice Court, I realized that I already was. I was in a group with the Father, Son, and Holy Spirit, and who could have more faith than they? I learned how important it is to form my beliefs by studying the Bible and what God has shown me along my journey and not from what others believe. The more I learned, the more my faith grew to believe I would see miracles if I kept praying. And so, I prayed to see my friend with multiple sclerosis healed along this journey to the greater life.

26 CONCEPT CROSSING

I'd often heard it said that seeing is believing. I've also learned in the kingdom of God quite the opposite to be true—believe and see. Although I'd already switched out many of those beliefs, my journey on Concept Crossing was to reveal a couple more from my childhood. Tracing where these old beliefs were formed and how they had shaped my life brought me to places I hadn't been before in Graceville. It took some courage to go there, but it turned out to be fun.

Oddly, something my new eye doctor said began my journey to Concept Crossing. During my first visit with him, while examining my eyes, he remarked that the vision in my left eye was significantly different than in my right eye. Yes, I told him, my left eye has been weak all my life. That's when he said something that fascinated me. He said, "Your left eye is only weak because your brain thinks it is."

That thought had never before entered my mind, and now it was all I could think about. Was it true, I wondered. It seemed reasonable; after all, my brain tells my body how to function, right? The concept was undoubtedly worth exploring, especially coming from a doctor. As a child, I remember an eye doctor saying my left eye was weak. Was that when the belief first started? I wore corrective glasses for a while, but they didn't seem to help. My right eye was strong, which made up for the weakness in the left eye, so I just accepted that was how I was. But now, I was wondering if I'd unnecessarily accepted it. Could changing how my brain thinks about it really improve the vision in that eye?

Applying the concept to improve my vision made me wonder what else I had accepted because of what someone said about me. I thought about being told by an elementary school teacher that I couldn't sing. I accepted it then, assuming some could sing, and some couldn't. But could it be that I can't sing because my brain thinks I can't sing because of what that teacher said? It's not surprising that a seven-year-old would believe what her teacher told her, but was it true?

Just for fun, I decided to do some investigating. I

emailed the worship leader at Bible study asking if she was born with a nice singing voice or if she learned to sing. She quickly wrote back, saying she'd been singing since childhood but that it could certainly be learned. She included the phone number of one of the women she sings with, saying she is a good voice teacher. I stared at that phone number and laughed. I told Jim about it, but he didn't think it was so funny. He actually encouraged me to call her. No, no, no, I told him, taking singing lessons would be like getting naked in front of a stranger, and there's no way I could do that!

God has a funny way of encouraging me, too. I did another book signing at my cousin's church, and there just happened to be a former worship pastor as a guest speaker that week. After service, my cousin invited Jim and me to lunch with them and the worship pastor. During lunch, the pastor asked if we had any questions he could answer. I couldn't help but ask the same question I asked my Bible study worship leader, "Can singing be learned, or is it a gift some are born with?" Before answering, he asked me to sing a little following along with him. Though he said it could be learned, the expression on his face after I sang told me it wasn't for everyone. So, I decided to give up the idea.

The following Sunday at our church, the sermon

was on the Last Supper. My pastor went on and on, describing how Jesus undressed Himself to wash the disciples' feet. Jim nudged me and whispered in my ear, "I know what you're thinking." At that moment, I knew there was no denying that God wanted me to take singing lessons. So, when we got home from church, I contacted the voice teacher my worship friend had recommended.

If, somehow, I could still think the events that led me to surrender to singing lessons were only a string of coincidences, what happened next put that notion to rest. I couldn't believe my ears when one of the location options to meet for my lessons was at my church! The voice teacher turned out to be the music teacher at the Christian middle school located at our church. That blew me away! How much more obvious can it get? The only way out of these lessons would be to say "no" to God, which would be even harder. We decided to meet during her lunch hour at church—so amazing!

In preparation for my first lesson, my teacher asked for a list of songs I wanted to learn. Throughout my life, I'd been uncomfortable having to sing even simple songs like "Happy Birthday," "Take Me Out to the Ball Game," and "Jingle Bells." Not to mention all the worship songs once I started attending church. Even not singing was uncomfortable at church, thinking others were noticing I wasn't singing. I would intentionally come late to avoid singing. When we became greeters, being outside during worship solved all those problems. Along with the list of songs, I was asked to bring a device to record my sessions so I could play them back during the week and practice between lessons.

Vulnerable, humbling, and weird might be some words to describe how I felt before the first lesson. Besides, I figured God must be up to something, considering all He did to get me there. The lessons began with some exercises to test out my voice. To measure my range, she had me scream as loud as I could, which came easy for me. She also said she could hear the range in my laugh, something else that comes easily. Holding my breath as long as I could wasn't hard either since I've always been a relatively good swimmer. Then came the part I'd feared for so long, but the courage I needed came. She played the piano, and together, we sang songs from my list, and before I knew it, our time was up. She said we could meet again the next week, but I wasn't sure I wanted to commit to every week. So, we decided on every other week and went from there.

We went at that pace for a couple of times. I learned some worship songs I was used to hearing at church and Bible study. It was challenging, but my voice was coming along, and it was starting to be fun. And then something happened that speeded up the whole process. I'll tell you about that next.

27 SINGING PLACE

I'd followed God into taking singing lessons, but I was getting the idea there was more to it than just learning to sing. As I turned onto Singing Place, I was reminded why I wanted to follow God. I was also given a compelling purpose that motivated me to do something I never imagined I would ever do. It was an unbelievable journey, and through it, I learned what it takes to do the uncomfortable things God leads me to do—what I've come to refer to as scary fun.

I started thinking I could learn to sing faster and surprise my teacher if I knew how to read music. Wrong! After watching a video on the subject, I was overwhelmed by how much there was to learn. I wanted to give up singing altogether, but my husband encouraged me to continue. Then, while listening to my recorded lesson, I heard my teacher say that she wasn't telling me a lot of technical stuff. She didn't want me to get caught up trying to remember it all and would instead guide me. She also explained that different tones come from my throat, chest, or stomach, which I hadn't understood before. Suddenly, all the testing and exercising of those parts of my body made sense. So, I decided to trust my teacher and let her guide me to what I'm ready to learn. After all, why would I want to learn on my own, anyway, when God had given me an excellent voice teacher?

More determined than ever to pay attention and do whatever my teacher told me, I prayed for her, and that God would guide her to what He wanted me to learn. I also bumped up my practice time between lessons. I'd listen to my session recordings daily, do all the exercises, and sing the songs. When I didn't understand something, I'd rewind and listen again or ask about it at my next lesson. My teacher was amazed that I was grasping complex concepts and how quickly I progressed. She kept saying I was progressing at the speed of light.

Seeing the difference a few lessons can make, I began getting the impression I was to encourage others who think they can't sing. I wasn't sure how that would come about until someone at Bible study asked me if I was going to sing at Sharing Day, which was just a few weeks away. "I've only had a couple of lessons, and I couldn't be ready to sing to anyone by that time," I told her, trying to put the scary thought out of my mind.

Then I realized I had already been singing to people. I'd been singing to the severely autistic man next door who screams and pounds on the wall so loud that I could hear him through my closed window. I thought if I could hear him, maybe he could hear me singing. So, I started opening my window when I practiced, hoping hearing words to worship songs like "Amazing Love" and "How Great is Our God" would give him peace. I started practicing on my walks and would sing to Jim and our dog, Sandy. One day at the cemetery, I sang "Amazing Grace" to Jim's mom, knowing it was her favorite song. It was a special moment, and it started me thinking if I was to get up the nerve to sing at Sharing Day, the first verse of "Amazing Grace" might be the way to go.

To get my teacher's thoughts on the idea, I emailed her about the impressions I was having. She replied, "Always using your gifts and stepping out in faith is a good idea." She also suggested I come for a lesson during the week and see where my heart settles afterward. I also shared what I was contemplating with my Bible teacher friend at our breakfast meeting. She has a beautiful singing voice and a lifetime of experience. I trusted her opinion, but I didn't think she would ask me to sing to her right there in the restaurant! I felt so naked that I covered myself with my arms and said, "No." When she kept insisting that I sing softly so only she could hear me, I finally gave in. She said I had a sweet, clear voice and encouraged me to sing at Sharing Day, even wishing she could be there. I didn't expect that! Taking another step, I asked my singing teacher if she thought I could be ready to sing the first verse of "Amazing Grace" by Sharing Day. She said the most amazing thing—yes! So, the race was on.

I started going weekly for a lesson, focusing on the first verse of "Amazing Grace." When I'd sung it correctly a few times while following my teacher and closely matching her sounds, she introduced a new concept—muscle memory. She had me sing it on my own, explaining that muscle memory would take over, and it would come out as I had practiced it. My teacher was amazed that I was singing a cappella with just a few lessons. It was so encouraging that I started working on the story I would tell before the song.

Our Bible study that year had been on the prophet Isaiah. I connected with Isaiah when I read that God had him go around preaching in the streets—naked! I'd also been learning about the righteousness of God, trying to grasp and accept that on the cross, Jesus exchanged His righteousness for my unrighteousness. I wasn't sure how to work that into the story until I'd gotten off-key singing for my teacher for the last time before the big day. My teacher helped fix it but finding out that muscle memory can fail freaked me out. I wanted to back out of the whole thing and probably would have if it wasn't for the message I had already prepared. Plus, I had invited my Bible teacher friend as my guest so she could see me sing. It all came into play as I walked up to the microphone in front of 190 women and began telling my story.

I began by saying I related to Isaiah when I read that God had him preach naked and that taking singing lessons made me feel the same way. I shared about an elementary school teacher who told me I couldn't sing. And how the question "Is singing a gift some are born with, or can it be learned?" had led me to singing lessons. After briefly telling some of what I'd learned, I planned to sing my song. Not sure how it would turn out, I prayed out loud, "I hope the Holy Spirit comes through for me right now. But whatever happens, I know that Jesus took His clothes off so I can be clothed with His righteousness, and that can never be taken from me. Thank You, Lord." Then I took a calming breath and out came "Amazing grace, how sweet the sound, that saved a wretch like me. I once was lost, but now I'm found, was blind, but now I see."

When I finished, everyone applauded. My teacher told me she was proud of me, and others were amazed at my courage. It was so scary; it was actually fun! The best part was when a young girl from the teen class came up to me and asked, "So it can be learned?" which told me I had accomplished my purpose. And for that, I was grateful.

28 PRECIOUS WAY

Amazed at what I'd done on Singing Place, I thought for sure the greater life I'd searched for was just around the corner. That was until I came to Precious Way, where I discovered there was more tucked away in my brain from childhood that was keeping me from the greater things to come. God had been making me aware of old beliefs, uprooting them one by one, and clearing the way for His power to work more fully in and through me. Another was revealed to me after God said something that took me a while to finally accept. Pieces from previous lessons came together to help me see why it was so hard to accept and why it was vital that I did.

One of the assignments in a series of classes Jim and I were taking at church called Rooted was to spend some quiet time in prayer and ask God if there was something He wanted to tell us. Then, we were to listen carefully for His response. Excitedly, I asked, "Lord, tell me something really good!" I hoped He would tell me something that would change the world, but instead, I heard, "You are precious in my eyes." As lovely as that was to hear, I was expecting something much more important. So, I asked, "Is there anything else, Lord?" but nothing else came.

Throughout my journey, God has shown His love for me. And although I was surprised to learn that God also honors me, I accepted it and now recognize those times more and more. But the thought that God sees me as precious was harder to accept. It just wasn't a word I would think to describe myself. I hadn't had a problem with the Bible verse in Isaiah, where God says, "You are precious in my eyes, honored, and I love you," because I took it to mean that we are all precious in His sight. But now God had said it to me personally, which made it harder for some reason, and I didn't know why.

After struggling with it for a while, I decided to believe it just because God said it. Jim got on board and changed his pet name for me from Pumpkin to Precious. He'd even call me from work just to tell me I'm precious. A friend I'd also told began referring to me as Precious when we talked, all to get me used to thinking of myself as precious.

God went about it differently, though. He began showing me evidence of how precious I am to Him. He helped me resolve something I'd long wondered about. It had to do with the woman at church who shared her son's suicide, which then began my journey with God. Her fear of where her son may have ended up caused me to rethink my plan and, instead, ask God to take me, which was the best decision of my life. For a long time, I struggled with why I was saved and not her son and so many others. I wasn't sure why I decided to finally ask, but I did. I asked, "Lord, why was my suicide plan redirected and not others?" He answered, "Because you are precious in my eyes." Then I asked, "But isn't everyone? Why weren't others saved like me?" He answered, "I couldn't make it known to them." I had to let that sink in, and when it did, I saw the importance of accepting how God sees me. I also saw how sharing it with others could possibly change the world. Still, God had more for me to see.

I was shown a different way of seeing Mary, the mother of Jesus. The Angel that announced she would give birth to the Son of God first started by telling her she was highly favored by God. I'd always thought Mary had to be someone special to be chosen for something so important. While still thinking about how highly favored Mary was, the Lord asked me a question that told me Mary wasn't the only one. He asked me, "What was the purpose of Jesus' birth, death, and resurrection?" I knew Jesus came to save us from our sins, but at that moment, I realized the reason why. Jesus came to save us—because we are all precious and highly favored by God. I was starting to accept it, but there was still more to know.

One Sunday, during silent prayer time at church, I heard, "I have marked you." "What?" I said. Then came, "As mine." I didn't know what that meant, and there wasn't time to think about it as the pastor continued his sermon. The answer came later while watching a pastor on TV, which I record and then watch after church each week. I wasn't paying much attention, though, until I heard the word "marked." He was explaining about being sealed or marked by the Holy Spirit as proof of God's possession. I couldn't help but wonder what the Lord was trying to tell me. At first, I thought it was about the sore I had gotten on my knee at the beach when I stumbled in the sand and fell on the pile of wood. The sore was in the shape of a wishbone. I thought it was kind of neat and didn't mind if it scarred. After watching the sermon again, I was given a clue. The Lord was strengthening my identity as His child to help me overcome the negative words spoken to me as a child. Still, I wasn't exactly sure what it all meant.

I'd always thought I had a relatively normal childhood. Sure, sometimes my parents got angry and would say some hurtful things they didn't mean, but I thought that happened to everyone. Plus, I thought I'd worked through and had forgiven all of that, but apparently, I'd missed something I didn't know about or didn't realize was important. That's when previous lessons began coming together to show me why I had so much trouble accepting that God sees me as precious. It turned out to be the same reason I had trouble believing that God could honor me or even love me—because I still believed the negative things said about me as a child. Without realizing it, those words had formed what I thought of myself. And what I thought of myself was overriding what God, or anyone, said about me. I began to understand that all I'd learned about God and what He could do through me was dependent on what I could see myself doing. And those negative thoughts still in my brain were blocking me from seeing myself doing anything greater than what I thought I could do.

After being shown my limiting self-image, where it had come from, and the power it still had in my life, I saw that it could be changed. So, my lesson on Precious Way was that I shouldn't judge how God sees me by how I think of myself. Instead, I should choose to believe what God says about me and allow that to change how I see myself. Changing how I view myself changes what I can do. And I'm excited to see what that will be!

29 PROTECTION BELTWAY

With powerful lessons still circulating through my mind from Precious Way, God gave me something new to think about. He said, "Many have pondered, but few have seen the miraculous view of heaven." At first, I thought the greater life of miracles I'd been wanting to see was about to begin. The more I thought about it, though, the more I wondered what He meant by "the miraculous view of heaven." So, I asked, "What does that mean, Lord?" His answer only made me more curious. All He said was, "You're on the right track." Protection Beltway seemed like a collection of unrelated experiences. Still, by the time I made my way around, I'd come to a greater understanding of the miraculous view of heaven.

The Lord was still pointing out things I trusted instead of Him. He caught me with another one shortly after our dog, Sandy, died. Without Sandy to protect me, I began feeling a little insecure about being home alone. I hadn't realized it until one day while locking our bedroom window, I felt the Lord say, "Why would you not think I would protect you?" It was a good question, so I asked myself, "Yeah, why would I not think God would protect me?" Thinking back over the previous week, I remembered sermons I'd seen on God's protection and suspected they had been for this moment. So, I went back and watched those sermons again. I also read books on God's promises of protection, others on angels and their role in protecting us, and Psalm 91 from the Bible.

Further around the Beltway came an experience that showed me how judging can get me off track. After church one Sunday, Jim and I stopped at the grocery store to pick up a few things. While waiting to check out, I noticed the only thing the woman in front of us had on the conveyor belt was a bunch of roses. *How fun,* I thought, and then said, "Oh, someone's getting roses!" The woman looked at me and said, "I'm visiting the cemetery for Halloween." All kinds of weird thoughts flooded my mind at that point. Yet, I had just come from a sermon on judging, so I only said, "Oh?" Then, the woman explained that her mother lived to be 95 years old and loved to give out candy to the children on Halloween. That's why she chooses to visit the cemetery on Halloween. Because I didn't judge, I was able to share a special moment with a stranger in the grocery store, both teary-eyed as she remembered her mother.

God spoke something else to me that let me know He was helping me to stay on track. During a discussion in my Bible study group about Eve wanting to be like God, I said, "She was already like God, just didn't know it." My group leader quickly added, "No one can be at the same level as God because He created us." I agreed, and the conversation ended. Later, I felt the Lord say to me, "Don't worry about being too much like Me; you can't. Worry more about not being enough like Me." I admit, at times, I had worried about making the same mistake as Eve. Relieved to know I couldn't, I became more confident in my desire to do the works of Jesus.

While packing the Christmas decorations, one of the ceramic choir boys I inherited from my mother fell off the shelf and shattered into several pieces. I was heartbroken. The choir boys meant the most to me of all my mother had given me over the years. I remembered how precious they were to her. As a child, I watched how carefully she wrapped each and packed them away for the following year. When I saw Jim picking up the broken pieces, I knew he would try to glue them together. I told him I didn't want to keep broken stuff glued together and begged him to throw them away, which he promised to do. Later, he confessed to digging them back out of the trash and piecing them together so he could search for one on eBay. And he had found one just like it. "I already let it go," I told him, "and will be happy with the two left." He said he'd seen the disappointment on my face and wanted to buy it to complete the set from my mom. Sometimes, I'm overwhelmed by how much my husband will do to make me happy.

When the choir boy arrived in the mail, Jim and I had a special moment as we carefully unpacked and looked him over. He was perfect. Jim said, "Your mom is smiling right now." Since all the other decorations had already been put away, we decided to keep the new choir boy out and enjoy him during the year. And so, I put him on the shelf in the dining room. And Jim moved him a little farther back on the shelf.

I received some insight after I started having pain in my left heel. I prayed and believed that my foot was healed by Jesus' wounds, but the pain persisted. Even the heel and arch support inserts I put in my shoes hadn't worked. While talking to God, I asked, "Lord, I know my feet have been healed by Jesus' wounds, so why hasn't my healing manifested? What do I need to do?" In Joseph Prince's book *The Prayer of Protection,* I read that God has provided everything, but what we receive depends on how much we think God loves us. The more we know how much God loves us, the more we will receive from Him. What I read resonated with me since my lessons from Precious Way had been about increasing my knowledge of how much God loves me. It also told me I wasn't trusting God to protect me because I still didn't know how much He loved me. Then my mind went to the broken choir boy. I thought about how I wouldn't accept it glued together and that Jim bought me one just like it, whole and new, and then I realized—that's what God did for us!

To receive more of what God has promised, I was led to an even deeper understanding of how much God loves me. The broken choir boy showed me a different way of looking at my new birth in Christ. I saw that I'm not broken and pieced together like I once thought. Instead, like the new choir boy, I am whole and new. God loves us so much that He couldn't leave us in our broken condition after Adam and Eve's fall and devised a plan to buy us back through His son, Jesus Christ.

Before coming to Protection Beltway, I thought that renewing my mind to God's thoughts and ways meant I was becoming a new creation. But now I see that it's already happened. The Bible says the moment I accepted Christ, I became a new creation, and the old has passed away. So, now that I understand my mind is being renewed to the knowledge that I'm already whole, I need to think of myself that way. Now that I have seen the miracle of my new birth from God's point of view, I wonder how different my life will look from here.

30 HUMBLE ALLEY

Have you ever gone from one place to another and later wondered how you got there? That's how my trip through Humble Alley turned out.

It was one of those times when you think you're doing something good, but it turns out to be wrong. I hadn't even realized what I'd done until I got a call from my higher-up at Bible study. I'd been researching using a wedge monitor for the worship team. They'd been saying it was hard to hear themselves sing, and a wedge monitor would help. I didn't know what a wedge monitor was, but after some research, I discovered that there were a couple among the equipment backstage. The problem was that neither my leader in the sound booth nor I knew how to connect them to the sound system. So, when our higher-up called, I thought she was calling to say the tech from the church would show us. Wrong! She was calling to tell me to drop the idea. She thought they were too heavy for us and feared we'd get hurt. She wasn't happy about me pushing for it either. Hoping to smooth things over, I told her I asked my study group if anyone was interested in helping in the sound booth, and one was. I thought she'd be happy to have some extra help. Wrong! Instead, in a serious tone, she said, "That's not the way we do things." I was so surprised by her response. After I hung up the phone, I felt so bad. I prayed and fought feelings of resentment.

The following day, I was still feeling bad about it all. After some thought, I knew it wasn't the way they did things. It wasn't how I'd gotten there. When I was approached, I was told my name came up after they prayed, so I accepted the position, believing it was what God had for me to do. It was also why I wanted to do a good job. Now I'd gone and gotten myself in trouble. Then I felt the Lord say, "So, how bad were you?" I love how He speaks to me. I smiled and thought, *Yeah, how bad was I? I was only trying to help, and what harm did I do anyway?* I felt better about it, but I still wasn't thrilled about going back. Then, something in a book I was reading spoke to me. It talked about being faithful and how God would promote you. I also received encouraging words from the worship leader after telling her there would be no wedge monitor. She also gave me more to think about when she said, "It's just a part of our learning how to relate and operate within the body of Christ." So, I decided to go back and see what God would do.

As I stood in the sound booth, looking down over the auditorium, watching those preparing for the morning to begin, I started to appreciate things I hadn't thought much about before. I thought about how much time the worship team spent praying, deciding on songs to sing, and rehearsing each week. I saw how faithful and devoted they were in what they did. I saw the teaching director and thought about the love she expressed through her lectures, always thinking of what God had given her to share with the ladies who came to learn. I thought about all the group leaders and their time preparing for each week's lesson. Then I thought about why I was there. And that's when it became clear—I was there to support all of them. I don't know why I hadn't seen it before, but I suddenly saw how my role in setting up the microphones and sound system was vital to everything they did. At that moment, I submitted, in my heart, to God and those He had placed over me. I said, "Okay, Lord, I'll do this. I want to be a part of what You are doing here." I found it interesting that the associate teaching director complimented me on my diligence and faithfulness minutes after surrendering. I took it to mean that God was pleased with my new commitment; it made me feel good.

It was a humbling experience. Everything seemed to change after that. I felt like I was in a different place, though the situation hadn't changed. It was I that changed. I was different, and it made a difference in what I did.

The more I began to concentrate on serving, mainly those with a microphone, the better I got. I gave more thought to the little details that made them feel cared for. Instead of just putting out the equipment, I started taking the time to set the mic stands to each one's height in the worship team and for the opening speaker. One of the things I started doing for the teaching director was quickly turning off her mic when she had to cough. During her lecture, I sat with my finger over the switch, looking for any little facial movement that signaled she needed to cough, sneeze, or get a sip of water. By studying her each week, I got to know her and got good at hitting the off button at the exact time, so her cough wasn't amplified and then back on just as she spoke her next word. It didn't go unnoticed; people started commenting on my precision. I began to think of it as an important thing I was doing. I saw it as my part in helping her feel confident as she stood on stage each week and delivered what God had given her to say.

Humility wasn't a fun lesson. It wasn't easy to go back to Bible study after being scolded for trying to help, but I'm so glad I did. So much good came from it. My purpose had become clear and more meaningful. After I humbled myself and renewed my commitment to God, I was reminded who my higher-up really is—the Lord Jesus Christ. Acting on the clue from my worship leader friend, I spent some time thinking about how the body of Christ operates. It was easier to understand if I related it to my body and how it works. Like my body, Christ's body is made up of many members, each working together with a specific purpose and abilities. If one part isn't doing what it should or tries to do someone else's part, as I did, the entire body suffers. Some members may seem more important than others, but the body won't function properly unless they all work together, which means all the members are important.

When I first found myself in Humble Alley, it didn't

seem like I'd end up feeling important. So, how did I get there? Humility! I had a new understanding of humility. It isn't weak or thinking less of myself like I once thought. It's more like a means of getting from one place to another. Humility had brought me to know my purpose, and knowing my purpose brought me to a place of confidence. I didn't feel the need to compete or defend myself as much, which brought me to a peaceful place. I started to like myself and to enjoy encouraging others. Thinking of myself as a member of the body has helped me get along better with others and even appreciate our differences. And oh, a little way down the road, I discovered that God does promote the faithful.

31 HIGHER POINT

I wasn't sure what I was hoping for when I signed up Jim and myself for a faith conference coming to our city. Mostly, I wanted to see something I'd only read about and seen so far on TV—a miracle. I had no idea what I would hear in the first few minutes would prepare and guide me through a tough time that I didn't know was coming.

On our way to the conference, in my mind, I was going over activities I'd considered cutting from my schedule. With all the things I had going, I felt I wasn't doing anything well. Some on the list were big things that needed Jim's input. I'm not sure why I thought the short drive to the conference would be a good time to discuss them with him, but I did. Casually, I asked, "Should we be spending so much time and money on our house right now?" After briefly listing a few other things, I progressed to the biggy, "Should I retire my business?" Knowing it was a lot to consider, I let him know I wasn't expecting an answer. At that point, I was only sharing my thoughts. When we arrived at the convention center and found a parking space, Jim took my hand and suggested we ask God what He would have us cut from my list. So, we prayed and quickly asked God for His priorities. The answer also came quickly.

At the conference, the opening speaker announced that he'd recently become the ministry's CEO and shared how overwhelmed he was feeling with all there was to do. I was already relating, but then he said, "And our properties are all in need of repair!" That really got my attention. Then he shared the answer he got after praying for priorities, "Don't cut anything; come up to a higher level of faith. And get your house in order!" is what the Lord told him. Jim and I looked at each other in amazement and agreed it was our answer, too!

Knowing that faith comes by hearing and hearing by the word of God, I decided to make my Bible study a priority. In fact, I added two more Bible studies I felt the Lord had led me to. When the studies began to be too much to do during the week, instead of letting some questions slide and only completing what I had time for, I committed to finishing them all, believing it would bring me to a higher level of faith and that everything would get done. I also asked my study groups to pray that I could keep that commitment. We also continued fixing up our house.

With all the Bible studies, I was learning so much, and my faith was growing. I was praying more and even learning through my prayers. Jim was due for the blood test that checked if cancer had returned, and before he left, I prayed the test would prove that by Jesus' stripes, he was healed. While saying goodbye, a correction to my prayer came to my mind. So, I told him, "It's not your blood that proves you're healed—it's Jesus' blood." After Jim left, another correction came to me. Again, I prayed, "Lord, Your blood proved Your word that says by Your stripes Jim is healed. And Your resurrection is proof that all of that is true!"

One of the new Bible groups I had joined decided their next study would be about heaven. They looked forward to knowing more about where they were headed, but I wasn't all that excited about it. I was more interested in learning how to bring heaven to earth as Jesus prayed in the Lord's prayer. Since I'd completed the one study, I thought it was a good time to step out of that group. That decision was turned around the following morning while watching a preacher on TV, talking about thinking small. "You gotta think bigger," he said. I'd heard that kind of thing before, but what he said next was a game-changer for me. He said, "Stop trying to bring God's plan down to your level. Let God take you up to His level." Wow, I felt like God was saying to me, "How do you think you can bring heaven to earth without first knowing what heaven is like?" He had me on that one!

Two days after deciding to stay and study heaven, my best friend's daughter called and told me her mom had died. It was so hard to believe. My friend couldn't have died so suddenly at age 64. I didn't want it to be true and hoped it was a terrible dream I'd wake up from. About an hour later, the thought came to me—*Why didn't I have Sarah put the phone up to Barb's ear so I could tell her to get up in the name of Jesus?* I hadn't even thought of it. When I told Jim it was because I didn't have the faith, he said, "You have the faith now; do it now." "But Sarah might not still be there, or they may have taken Barb already," I answered. "Find out," he said, "Call her." I didn't know if it would work out, and Sarah might think I was crazy, but with Jim's encouragement, I called Sarah back. She answered and was still at the hospital outside the room where her mother lay. I asked if she would put the phone to her mother's ear. She didn't comment or ask any questions, as I feared. She only said she had to get someone to let her in. Surprisingly, it only took a few minutes, and she had the phone to my friend's ear. I had the chance, so boldly, I said, Barbara Lynn—get up in the name of Jesus! I said it a couple of times and then asked Sarah if her mom woke up. "No," Sarah said. My friend didn't get up, but I was glad I gave her that chance. Though delayed, I was also glad to have had the faith to think of it.

Thinking it might cheer me up, I did the greeting at church that Sunday as if nothing happened. I was doing pretty well until one lady asked how my week went, and I said, "Oh, not so good, actually." I said it in a way most would have nodded in sympathy, but not this lady. She looked me in the eye and asked what was going on. So, I told her my best friend of fifty years had died suddenly on Friday. Then she pulled me aside and said something my friend would have said as she hugged me, "Oh honey, I'm so sorry." I cried; she also cried and held me until she thought I was okay to return to greeting. I guess it was what I needed. Thank You, Lord.

Jim and I drove to Texas for the funeral. While there,

I was glad to have a quiet moment to explain to Sarah about putting the phone to her mother's ear. "Everyone has a different way of coping," she said. When I told her what I'd said, she seemed to like it, even believing it could have happened, and was glad I'd given her mom that chance. I was happy to hear her say her mom would have wanted to come back to life. Some don't, I'm told.

I thought I'd have a friend who could tell me firsthand what heaven is like, but that didn't happen. Still, learning more about where my friend is and what she's doing made studying heaven much more interesting.

32 COURAGE RIDGE

Three weeks after my friend died, I was given another opportunity to pray and raise someone from the dead. A deputy called and told me that my brother, Tom, had been killed by a drunk driver and that she was in custody. It seemed unreal, so close to hearing about Barbara and now Tom. After a few hours in shock, my faith again rose up. I prayed out loud in the name of Jesus for Tom to get up, to live, and not die. Then I waited to hear. It was winter on the mountain where Tom had made his life, and his friends there had decided to wait until Spring to hold a memorial service. God used the time in between to show me more about bringing heaven to earth and how courage works with faith.

I had no doubt Barbara was in heaven, but I wasn't as sure about Tom. I knew he believed in God from the one time he told me that God has always existed. Still, I didn't know what he understood about Jesus and if he'd accepted Him. So, I asked God if Tom had made it to heaven. The answer came while talking with our cousin, Pastor Linda. I told her about all the time I had spent with Tom getting our parents' house ready for sale, how he allowed me to lay hands on his various pains and pray for his healing, and that he believed it would help him. Then Linda told me about what Jesus said to his disciples in Matthew 10:40, "He who receives you receives Me, and he who receives Me receives Him who sent Me." That was my answer! Tommy was in heaven!

Feeling the power of my friends' prayers, I continued with my Bible study commitments. I thought I was doing well until I realized I hadn't set up a mic stand for one of the worship singers. Seeing that I wasn't functioning as well as I thought was eerie. While talking with the worship leader, I told her I had no anger or resentment toward the drunk driver. Then she said something I never saw coming. She said she saw the woman reading my book. *Wow,* I thought, *I don't know if I'm that far along.* My leader in the sound booth also told me something I didn't think I was quite ready for. She told me about a California law that gives the victim's family the right to speak at the sentencing. The thought of standing up in court and sharing my feelings made me nervous, but it was almost like the Lord was preparing me for it. So, I decided to pray for the words He would have me say.

The words for the Victim Impact Statement turned out to be pretty much what I was feeling and settled a question that had bothered me. I wondered how I could forgive the woman and yet want her prosecuted for what she'd done. The statement briefly said, "I have a conflict of interest in this case and should probably recuse myself. As a Christian, I am commanded to forgive you. And I have. Under God, through the blood of Jesus Christ, all have been forgiven, so who am I not to forgive? But at the same time, your reckless actions are responsible for my brother's violent death. And so, while I hold no malice toward you, I will in no way interfere with these legal proceedings and will let justice take its course. I'll continue to pray for you to come to the knowledge and forgiveness that Jesus offers you and that your life may come of good to others. Thank you for this opportunity to speak."

My leader thought my statement was very good. I did, too, which gave me the confidence I thought I'd need to say it in court. Still, as the trial date kept getting postponed for various reasons, I began to lose courage. Although I understood the role of forgiveness, I didn't think it would go down easily for those around me who were still angry and bitter. Learning to forgive has been a large part of my journey. In my book, *A Different Way,* two chapters were dedicated to forgiving and the life-changing benefits I experienced from it. Since then, I've come to believe forgiveness is God's plan for bringing heaven to earth and that it's all laid out in the Lord's prayer.

So many of Tom's friends showed up to the memorial service. I enjoyed hearing about their special times with Tom and those who spoke of how he had helped them. I wasn't sure if they'd be interested in knowing that Tom made it to heaven, but it was what I wanted to share if I were to muster up the courage. While sitting with my other two brothers, one started talking about when Tom was home helping clean out our parents' house, and I just knew it was my cue from the Lord. Nervously, I stepped up to the microphone, said I was Tom's sister, and wanted to share a story. It was tough to back out at that point, so I started telling them that Tom and I spent a lot of time together, preparing our family home for sale. I shared that I'd discovered God later in life and had become interested in the healing Jesus provided for us. I told of the various pains Tom would come with, and when I'd ask if I could lay hands on him and pray, he always said yes. They laughed when I told of the time he had a toothache, and his cheek was all swelled up, and when I asked if I could pray for him, he said, "Yeah, but don't touch it!" Then I told them I'd asked God if he made it to heaven and how the answer had come. I ended with, "If it matters to you, I wanted to share that Tom is in heaven." When I finished, a couple came and hugged me, thanked me for sharing, and said they were glad to know that Tom was in heaven.

I was glad to have had the courage to share my story and learn more about Tom from his friends. He'd moved away from our family home so long ago and lived a different life than we were raised. I was glad to know he was happy in the mountain life he had found. As I write this, it's been almost three years since the awful crash. The woman is still in jail awaiting her trial, and I've had plenty of time to grow into the impact statement the Lord gave me. I learned that I could trust courage to be there when I stepped toward it. Just like when I stepped up to share my faith at the memorial service and courage came, I can trust it will be there when it's time to stand up in court and share the

Victim's Impact Statement. And maybe I'll also have the courage to give the woman my book to fulfill my worship friend's vision.

33 MOCK BYWAY

My cousin, Pastor Linda, had gone with Jim and me to Tom's memorial service and spoke there about forgiveness. On the way home, out of the blue, she told me I was a genius. Thinking she was kidding, I laughed and said, "That's crazy!" She was serious, though, and kind of upset that I would laugh. She then told me to stop mocking her. I didn't say anything more about it, but I still didn't believe her.

The following day, still thinking about it, I searched my mind to see what about me would make Linda believe I was a genius. That's when the Lord said I do the same thing with Him—mock Him when I don't believe what He says about me. *Wow,* I thought, *now that's really serious!* "You have my attention, Lord," I said. Then, He related it to healing. Instead of accepting by faith that I'm healed by His stripes, he told me I search my body and other places for proof that I'm healed. I saw His point. I was doing the same thing by looking for evidence that I was a genius instead of accepting the words given to me by faith.

First Linda, and then the Lord, saying I mock them? There must be something to it, but what exactly, I wasn't sure. It seemed a lot similar to when I had trouble accepting that I'm precious in God's eyes. So, I went back and reread my Precious Way blog. Seeing the lessons there made me think this could be a test, a continuation, or possibly both. I had learned negative words spoken over me as a child can override what God or anyone says about me. Which makes it difficult to see myself doing anything greater than what I was told. My conclusion on Precious Way was that I shouldn't judge how God sees me by what I think of myself but instead, allow what God says about me to change how I see myself. Putting together what I'd been told so far on Mock Byway, I thought I might begin to see miracles if I accepted what God says about me. So, excitedly, I followed along to see what else I'd learn.

I wouldn't have gone looking to learn about insecurity. But Beth Moore's book, *So Long Insecurity,* found me at church one morning. When we arrived to greet, there were tables full of books on the patio. The church library was closing, and they were giving all the books away. We were told to take a look to see if there were any we wanted. I looked through the books, and *So Long Insecurity* was the only book that interested me. Still, I wasn't sure I'd read it. I like Beth Moore a lot. She's fun to watch, but I feared I might get frustrated reading through her flowery stories to get to the meaty insights I really like. I had the time while waiting for books I'd ordered to come, and it was free, so I thought I'd see what it was about.

I was surprised at how much I got out of it. Beth explained what insecurity is, where it comes from, and how it steals our peace and joy and limits what God can do through us. I didn't want that! I wondered if it could be why I wasn't seeing healing miracles. It also made me wonder how I'd be able to do genius-level things while rejecting the thought of being a genius. My thinking was challenged when I read, "Fear of the future makes people settle for things in the present that completely defy abundant life. It also insults the grace of God that will be piled in heaps for us when hardship comes." This line I read a few times and then wanted to write it on my wall... "The Creator of heaven and earth assigned us dignity and immeasurable value, and only when we finally accept those inalienable truths will we discover authentic security." And this sentence said it all, at least for me: "In the radiance of His greatness, we are made great."

Soon after finishing *So Long Insecurity,* I received the book I'd anxiously awaited—*Accelerated Healing* by John Proodian. I'd seen the author interviewed on TV and was intrigued by his story. He was a pastor and prayed for people to be healed but saw no one healed in thirty years. He'd gotten to the point he was afraid to pray for people. When his wife needed prayer for her knee, they went to a healing conference. While his wife received healing, he received faith for a healing ministry when a 12-year-old girl, the size of a five-year-old, grew to normal size right before their eyes! How I'd love to see a miracle like that! Yet, there was more in the book to help develop my faith for healing. I found this to be a powerful statement, "If one understood and truly believed that Christ was in them, they'd never be afraid to lay hands on someone. And to not see that person healed would never enter into their thinking because, hey, Christ is in them." *Accelerated Healing* was so powerful that I read it twice before passing it on to a friend. And reread it when she returned it a couple of weeks later.

The lessons on Mock Byway came together while

we were traveling on a train through Alaska. The tour guide was pointing out glaciers, but I couldn't see them. I was so confused. I expected to see a glacier in the water, but we were looking at mountains. The guide explained that glaciers are formed on the sides of mountains and eventually slide down into the water. When I heard the man next to me say, "I guess I need to redefine my idea of a glacier," I knew I did, too. And not just for glaciers. I needed to redefine my idea of myself. I always thought a genius was a brilliant person, much more intelligent than me. What I wasn't taking into account was the Holy Spirit inside me. I needed to seriously start thinking of myself as not only me but Jesus and me together in everything I do and see what happens.

34 MIRACLE MILE

When Jim and I returned from Alaska, I learned my friend, Debra, had received the miracle many had prayed for. She'd been healed from the incurable disease multiple sclerosis! Though it came suddenly, it was a long twenty-five-year journey getting there.

My friendship with Debra, the worship leader at Bible study, began about three years before her miracle healing when I joined the tech team. I got to know her and the disease she'd been living with through short chats while setting up and putting away the sound equipment. I learned that she needed to sit while she played the guitar and sang to conserve her strength. After she explained that the higher stool allowed her the lung capacity to sing, I made sure to always have one set out for her. I also discovered we had something in common that not many do. She, too, has written a book, *Garden Lessons,* and writes a blog based on her experiences with God.

Debra didn't seem to mind my questions about her illness or ones regarding divine healing. At one point, I asked her the same question Jesus asked the lame man who had been waiting at the pool for 38 years to be healed, "Do you want to be made well?" Immediately, she replied, "Yes!" But then said that God would heal her in His time. And in the meantime, she's learning much and becoming closer to the Lord. It was almost as if she didn't mind living with multiple sclerosis. But I minded. I wanted her to be well and believed she could be. I also asked what I knew to be another important question in receiving God's healing, "Do you have unforgiveness toward anyone?" She assured me she didn't.

As our friendship developed, we began sharing more about our lives through Facebook messaging, emails, and two-hour lunches. Debra's been a Christian all her life; her father was a pastor, and she's studied the Bible for so much longer than I have. Her feedback meant a lot to me. It also, at times, revealed differences in our beliefs, like the one time, I told her I was praying for her healing, and she said she'd take it if that was the Lord's will for her. When I replied, "It is His will, why would you say 'If'?" she answered, "Because He has said no for 23 years." I could see how it would look like a "no," but I had trouble believing God would say "no" when Jesus shed His blood for our healing.

Though I prayed for symptoms to be healed as she'd tell me about them, I'd wanted to lay hands on her and pray she'd be healed from multiple sclerosis, but I just wasn't sure how to approach her about it. About two years before her miracle, the opportunity presented itself in the most unlikely way—while I was driving! While riding home together from the weekend Bible study retreat, I suddenly asked if I could lay my hands on her and pray. She agreed, so I reached over and touched her and said a quick prayer for her to be healed from multiple sclerosis in Jesus' name. We were both amazed at how it came about and believed Jesus had healed her. Later, I messaged to tell her I was fully convinced that Jesus can, will, and has healed her from multiple sclerosis. She agreed but added something that prompted me to start doing more than pray for her. She said, "And Lord grow my faith!"

At the time, I'd been growing my faith for Jim's healing from cancer and thought of all the books I'd read about God's healing. I remembered the collection of *Healing Journeys* DVDs from Andrew Wommack

Ministries I had and how much seeing them had boosted our faith. Thinking they might help grow Debra's faith for healing, I asked if she'd be interested in watching actual people who've been healed tell how their healing came about. She said she was. So, I brought one to Bible study the next week, and we exchanged them each week or so as she was ready for another.

Questions over the DVDs led us to some interesting conversations and sometimes into conflicts over our different beliefs. Conflicts seemed to center on her belief that God was allowing the disease to teach and grow her. My thinking was that her faith was divided between believing God was using the disease to bless her and believing He was healing her. When I told her God had no reason to allow a disease that Jesus had defeated with His blood, it didn't sit well with her. I was sent a long list of blessings she had received over the twenty-four years, along with supportive scripture. I felt bad about upsetting her but was glad to learn more about what she believed and why. I looked up all the scriptures she included and saw some that supported my beliefs, too.

Even though I told her I would still believe that Jesus healed her when He took the stripes on Himself, she was convincing in her beliefs. I began to have doubts and got frustrated trying to make sense of all that she kept telling me and comparing it to what I'd been learning about healing. Confused and frustrated, I gave it all to God. I said, Lord, Debra's right; if she's going to be healed, then You will do it. I can't make it happen for her; maybe I'm trying to do something that isn't up to me. So, I give it all to You, Lord.

After my rant, I was reminded that I shouldn't base my beliefs on what others say. I need to establish what I believe in what God's word says to me. I also noticed an encouraging change in Debra's words to me. She said, "The DVDs are giving me much to ponder and pray about! I'm listening for God's voice and having some interesting conversations. So, stay tuned! I know healing is coming!" When she finished with all the DVDs, we began exchanging books we were reading. The last one I gave her was the book *Accelerated Healing* by John Proodian.

It came to the point where all the medications Debra had been taking to control the multiple sclerosis symptoms began causing other problems in her body. So, to cleanse her system, her doctor took her off everything, which then caused a bad multiple sclerosis flare-up. While praying and worshiping, she cried out for Jesus to heal her. She said she instantly felt something in her legs and has been strong and normal ever since. Hallelujah! Wow! Glory to God!

Three years since her healing, I'm witnessing a miracle each time I see Debra standing strong to play her guitar and sing, no longer needing to sit on a stool! She is no longer like the lame man at the pool waiting to be healed. I now see her as the woman in the Bible who came to Jesus saying, "If only I touch His garment, I will be made well." When she did, the woman immediately felt in her body that she was healed. And Jesus said to her, "Daughter, your faith has made you well."

35 AUTHORITY PASS

Authority was not a subject that interested me until I saw its connection to great faith. When I was writing Humble Alley, the Lord had me reread the Bible story of the centurion who came to Jesus seeking healing for his paralyzed servant. Other times, my focus had been on Jesus, marveling at the centurion's great faith because I was hoping for that. This time, I saw the centurion's humility when, even though Jesus said he would come and heal his servant, he said, "Lord, I am not worthy that You should come under my roof." I wanted to share how I'd made the connection between great faith and humility then. Still, I waited because I'd also seen another connection to great faith—the understanding of authority.

The centurion believed Jesus didn't need to actually come to heal his servant. He told Jesus, "But only speak a word, and my servant will be healed." He then explained why he believed, "For I also am a man under authority, having soldiers under me. And I say to this one, 'Go,' and he goes; and to another, 'Come,' and he comes; and to my servant, 'Do this,' and he does it." It was the centurion's understanding of authority that caused Jesus to marvel. In Authority Pass, I was given my own understanding of authority. It came through a powerful word from the Lord, a promotion, and a new way of looking at authority.

Before going to our Bible study group, my leader in the sound booth, Shelley, and I set up the microphones, ready for the children's ministry performance. On my way back to the sound booth after group, Nancy, our higher-up, mentioned that she had readjusted the microphones according to the children's director's instructions. While the children were taking their places on stage, one of the teachers came to the sound booth and told Shelley and me that the microphones weren't set up correctly for the children. As she started to tell us how they should be, I spoke up and said, "Nancy has them set to Barb's instructions." The teacher stopped and said, "Ok, that settles it." She then turned and walked away. Wow, that was easy, I said, as Shelley and I looked at each other, amazed at how quickly she agreed.

Later that night, as I was falling asleep, I wondered what caused the teacher to quickly surrender her plan. Thinking it had something to do with the children's director having more authority than the teacher, I concluded that it was the use of Barb's name. I also thought if Nancy hadn't told me she had adjusted the microphones to Barb's instructions, who knows how it could have turned out. That's when I felt the Lord say, "It should work the same with My Name." Wow! Immediately, I knew I'd been given a powerful lesson.

The authority lessons continued in a more practical sense when I received a promotion. Near the end of the year, Nancy and Shelley told me they would not be returning to Bible study the following year due to personal life changes. What? But that would mean I'd be the only one left who knew anything! Don't worry, they said, they would train someone to work with me, which they did. They trained three. One was to replace Nancy, and two were in Shelley's place to work with me in the sound booth.

When the new year began, I was invited to join the leaders' group. *How fun,* I thought, *to be back in the leaders' group, where I learned so much during the two years as a children's teacher.* I hadn't yet put it together that I was the new leader in the sound booth. I didn't actually find out until I was introduced to the group as the new lead tech. I was so surprised; I didn't know what to say. So, what I was thinking just came out of my mouth, "I didn't know I was lead tech! I thought I was co-tech!" And everyone laughed. Afterward, I remembered, tucked amidst the tough lessons on humility, I'd learned that the Lord promotes the faithful. At the time, I hadn't considered it much more than motivation for making my way through Humble Alley, but suddenly, there it was.

Another lesson came while listening to Curry Blake's CD on *the Authority of the Kingdom.* I thought I knew what authority was, but Curry renamed it in such a way that made it abundantly clear to me. When he said that authority is nothing more than "Pre-Permission," I understood it completely. A couple of days before, a client had given me pre-permission to decide how many of his prescription forms to order. I'd worked many years with this client, always giving him price quotes for three quantity breaks, as was my custom. He was in a rush for them this time and was so busy that he didn't have time to talk. He asked me to go by what he ordered last time and to order the best quantity pricing. He specifically said he was giving me permission ahead of time, and I didn't need to run it by him for approval. He was giving his approval now while talking to me. Having that experience made it easier to understand what Curry Blake was saying when he said, "Each time we see a sick person, we don't need to ask permission to pray. Jesus already gave pre-permission when He said, 'Believers shall lay hands on the sick, and they shall recover.'"

A test of the pre-permission lesson came during my new position as the lead tech. The ear hook microphone used by the teaching director was intermittently tuning in and out, and I thought we should buy a new one to have as a backup. Thinking the clip-on lapel mic would be more convenient for guest speakers, I emailed the teaching director a link to the one I had in mind. She replied that she prefers the ear style but trusts me and to go ahead and order what I think is best. Even though I thought the clip-on mic would be best, wanting to please the director, I ordered the ear mic she preferred, which turned out to be a mistake. After using the ear mic a few times, the director came to me and said that the ladies hugging her before her speech moved the microphone out of place. Thinking it may have been the problem with the old mic, she wanted to change to the lapel-style mic. I couldn't help thinking we would already have it if I'd done as I was told and ordered the mic I thought was best the first time, which led me to believe I needed to start trusting myself when others say they trust me.

The thought of Jesus trusting me with His name was, and still is, very humbling. But a greater understanding of authority increased my faith to begin exercising the authority I'd been given when praying in His name. My leadership role at Bible study would soon become even more significant in my life as my journey to great faith continued.

36 UNCOMMON PATH

When I'd supported others on their healing journey, it didn't seem that hard to see where they weren't trusting Jesus for His healing. However, it was more challenging when it came time to decide a path for my healing. Making decisions on my health not only actively challenged my faith but also helped me see where I was on my faith journey.

I'd been having pain in my left shoulder blade with tingling and numbness down my left arm. After praying and declaring my healing in Jesus' name for a couple of months, I finally told Jim about it. He then made an appointment with a chiropractor he'd gone to who'd been recommended by a friend. The evening before my appointment, a neighbor unexpectedly dropped in for a visit and updated us on his various medical issues. My interest peaked when he shared about needing neck surgery. When he described a pain that started in his neck and went down his left arm, I said I had the same thing. "That's not good," he said. He told us that when the pain started, he'd gone to a chiropractor, and the chiropractor got too strong and hurt him.

After our neighbor left, I thought it wasn't a coincidence he had dropped in and told us that story. Feeling it was the guidance I'd been looking for from God, I told Jim I didn't want to go to the chiropractor. He assured me his chiropractor was very gentle and wouldn't hurt me. So, again, I was open to the appointment until the following day when I heard Joyce Meyer on TV. She talked about how we ask God for guidance but aren't willing to do what He says out of fear of going against what others say.

Jim and I argued back and forth about it. When he again told me his chiropractor wouldn't hurt me, I told him God wouldn't hurt me either. He said the doctor could do one little tweak, and it would be gone. I said so could God. It could happen as soon as I choose God over the doctor. That's when I saw the crossroads and what Joyce was warning about. I was tempted to go to the chiropractor just to please Jim. *What would it hurt,* I thought. *It might hurt a lot, according to our neighbor.*

After explaining to Jim that I wanted to follow where I felt God was leading me, even if I was wrong, he said he would call and postpone my appointment.

Then, while at Bible study, my worship leader friend told me about a chiropractor who does what she called a one-finger touch treatment. She gave me his phone number and later sent me a link to his website. After checking it out, I felt it might be God's guidance. So, I made an appointment, and Jim came with me.

The doctor took x-rays and other tests that included comparing my leg lengths and a scan of my neck that produced a graph. My left leg turned out to be a half-inch shorter than my right, and my number one vertebra was out of alignment. He said it was probably from an old injury that hadn't healed correctly. He said he could put it in the correct position and that once it's back in place, my brain would flow correctly through my nervous system again, and my body would heal itself. That sounded good to me. Then he warned that it could be a lengthy process depending on how old my injury was. He explained that after he puts the vertebra in its correct position, it will want to go back to the place it's been used to for so long and that it takes a few times before it will stay. I would at first need to be checked twice a week, then less and less as it holds for longer periods. He also said it would heal faster if I didn't take any pain medication. I'd only been taking Advil, but he said he'd be opening up my nervous system, and medicine shuts it down by numbing the pain. After considering all the information, Jim and I agreed to proceed with the treatment plan.

It did turn out to be a long process. It was months before my neck started holding for extended periods and almost a year before the pain went away and I could return to all my regular activities. Getting there was a rough road, though. It seemed to get worse before it got better, and there were times I feared it wouldn't get better. As the pain in my back continued and my neck got stiffer, I started reducing activities, which ended up being just about everything. The one thing I felt I couldn't quit was Bible study until my newly formed tech team was ready to carry on without me. I often wondered if God had another reason for making it so I wouldn't leave Bible study. It was hard just getting up and dressed, let alone all I needed to do there, so I did take an Advil or two to help me through.

Concerned friends began advising various remedies that had worked for them, such as healing oils, pain patches, stretching exercises, and massages. When I asked the chiropractor about the different things, he'd say they wouldn't help and would only interfere with what he was doing. He kept reminding me that aligning my neck would allow my brain to flow through my nervous system normally, and my body would heal itself. It made complete sense to me, but when I tried to explain it to others, they didn't understand and would urge me to see a medical doctor. I was starting to see that my path was not for everyone, but it still seemed right for me.

I was glad Jim agreed and supported me. He had taken me to all my appointments and heard the information from the chiropractor firsthand. He even learned how to check my leg lengths and see whether my neck was out or holding before my checkups. Even with Jim's support, the pressure from well-meaning friends to get an MRI became overwhelming, and I gave in. I changed medical insurance to better cover the cost of an MRI, and by the time I saw a primary doctor in the new plan, I'd much improved. The doctor ordered X-rays, the same ones as the chiropractor, no MRI, and prescribed medication. She also told me to stop seeing the chiropractor until we see if the medicine helps or not. Again, I found myself at the crossroads, deciding whether to stay on the path with the chiropractor where I felt God had led me or switch to the course others had urged me to go. After thinking and praying about it, I decided I would not stop seeing the chiropractor since I was getting positive results.

I'd come to know I didn't yet have the faith to rely only on Jesus' name for my healing like I first wanted. But from the resistance, I could tell I was on an uncommon path, which I learned similarly takes faith. As I kept finding myself at a crossroads, I ultimately admitted that fear and doubt had brought me there. When I did, God said to me, "Now you know." Relieved, knowing God understood and forgave me, I continued with Him, and He removed the source of something holding me back. I'll tell you about that next.

37 EDIFICATION CORRIDOR

My journey from Uncommon Path had brought me to what I would describe as an in-between place, a corridor perhaps. God had shown me I wouldn't have been so easily swayed by others if it weren't for my fear and doubt. I thought if I had enough strength, I'd be able to stay on my path no matter what others said. But God, in His extraordinary wisdom, showed me how He can go about revealing and removing a cause of my fear and doubt.

Neck pain had caused me to quit just about everything in my life. The only thing I didn't quit was Bible study. If I could have, I certainly would have. But I'd become audio/visual tech leader after the two I'd worked with moved away, and I felt I had to stay and teach the two new ladies all I knew. Plus, I felt there may be another reason God had for keeping me there, and I was curious to know what it was.

With my neck finally holding in position, I was feeling better. So much so that I was starting to return to some of my regular activities. Since becoming tech leader, I hadn't attended the leaders' meetings on Wednesdays. I'd been saving all my energy for the regular Friday Bible study, where I was needed to lead my tech team. Now that I was better, I wanted to learn leadership skills to lead more successfully. I would never have thought a lesson on "edification" was what I really needed. I didn't even know what the word meant at the time. But as it turned out, it was God's lesson for me.

I couldn't believe the compliments I was getting on how well I was leading my tech team. Week after week, the leaders prayed and praised God for me. I kept telling them it wasn't me; it was the two amazing women assigned to help me, but they insisted it was my doing. I tried to accept it and be thankful, but inside, I thought, *That's crazy! I've only been trying to teach them everything I know as fast as possible so they can carry on without me if it comes to that!* Like a flood, the compliments continued, verbally and in handwritten cards and notes. I'd never gotten so many compliments. Yet, I wasn't feeling worthy of any. I sloughed them off, thinking they didn't really know me. Then, one morning, the Lord showed me what it was all about.

It was a difficult morning at Bible study when a particular event moved us to another part of the church from where we usually met. The equipment in that room was a little different. And though we'd met there before, it had been a while. Not only did I need to familiarize myself with the equipment there but I also had to quickly train my team. Working together, we found and set up the microphones and were able to get all of the screens working. The one thing we couldn't figure out was how to record. We always provided an audio file of the opening speaker and the teaching for those who couldn't attend. While my leader tried contacting a tech from the church to help us, my team and I continued trying everything we could think of. It was stressful, but in those moments when I felt like giving up, something remarkable happened. All those positive words and prayers the leaders spoke about me started running through my mind, encouraging me, and reminding me of how much they believed in my ability. I couldn't let them down. So, I kept going, and so did my team. We never figured out how to record through the soundboard but instead recorded on one of our phones, which worked well.

The following week, when the word "edification" appeared in our Bible lesson, I was curious about its meaning and looked it up in the dictionary. After reading the definition, I knew it was what I'd been experiencing! I was excited and wanted to share what I'd learned with the leaders who helped bring it about. And there happened to be a perfect question in our lesson for me to share what the Lord had taught me about edification. So, when that question came up at the following leaders' meeting, I put my hand up to answer. I shared how on Friday when things got difficult, all of their prayers and compliments started running through my mind, encouraging and keeping me going. I told them I'd had trouble accepting their edifying words about me because they didn't align with what I'd heard from my childhood. I began to cry as I told them that God was building me up and strengthening me to do things I didn't know how to do. As I continued through my tears, I could feel the woman beside me rubbing my back in gentle little circles. As comforting as it was, I later learned there was more to it.

Later, I talked to one of the leaders, telling her that the one beside me rubbed my back as I shared my story. She then said something that hadn't occurred to me.

She said, "That was God washing all those negative words spoken over you as a child from your heart!" I was so amazed! Was that from God, I wondered. Did God arrange for that woman to sit beside me and then rub my back? And then to give me the meaning of it through this other woman? Did He do all of that for me? I was curious to know for sure. So, I asked her if what she said was given to her by the Holy Spirit, and she said yes. When I asked the woman who had rubbed my back the same question, she said she had felt guided by the Spirit. It was another emotional time when I shared at the next leaders' meeting what the Lord had done for me right before our eyes and how they all had been a part of it.

My lesson in Edification Corridor wasn't a new lesson. Throughout my journey, I'd had trouble accepting complimentary words spoken about me. In various ways, God has shown me how He sees me and reminded me that's how He wants me to see myself. But I always seemed to go back to my old thinking. This time, I was given further understanding. I saw a clear difference in what I could do due to having positive thoughts about myself. Plus, I witnessed God's incredible leadership skills in action. I saw, firsthand, how He goes about leading others to accomplish His healing work in us. I couldn't have had a better leader to teach me leadership skills! Thank You, Lord!

38 REFLECTION CREEK

My desire to see God work through me seems to inspire some and worry others. Some say reading my journey to what I call *The Greater Life,* helps them see the possibilities of the power of Jesus in and through them. Some find my pursuit thought-provoking and challenging to their own pursuits in the Lord. Yet another one worries that my desire to do the works Jesus did may be misunderstood by some to mean that I want to be Jesus. I stopped to ponder these things after a friend asked me a question. She asked, "Is 'The Greater Life' a destination, or could it be this journey where God is granting your heart's desire? Might God want you to have an insatiable appetite for His greater good and higher purpose, at all times in all things while you're sojourning on this earth?" My first thought was that I'd already come to what I called "A Better Life" shortly after my journey began. So, if I got there, "The Greater Life" must be a destination too, right? As I reflected more on what my friends had to say, God continued teaching me, giving me even more to ponder.

I learned a more effectual way to pray while praying for my brother Glenn before he was taken to surgery. When I asked if I could pray for him, he agreed. So, I said a simple prayer, asking God to be with him and to see that everything goes perfectly well, and adding that there would be no pain. When I heard those words come out of my mouth, I thought, *Wait, what?! I just prayed for a painless surgery?* I didn't say anything, but while Jim and I were in the waiting room, I couldn't help thinking about the prayer. How crazy I thought it was, to pray for a painless surgery. How could there be such a thing? I knew Glenn had had the same surgery before and dreaded the pain. Even so, I could see myself praying for little or tolerable pain, but for no pain? That didn't seem like something I would think to pray. That's when I got the idea it was God. God had put those words in my mouth to pray!

Later, after the surgery, it didn't seem so crazy when my brother had no pain. Not when the anesthesia wore off. Not even after being moved to his room, did he want any pain medication. Nor when the physical therapist came to walk him around the hallways. I first suspected a miracle when the therapist was surprised that Glenn had no pain. When Glenn sat up in bed, swung his legs around the side, and stood up, the therapist said, "Wow, most guys would be doubled over in pain." That was when I was convinced it was a miracle.

When I shared the experience with a pastor at church, she confirmed my thinking that the words I spoke in my prayer were from the Holy Spirit. I was amazed at how easily the miracle came, yet there was something I still didn't understand. So, I asked, "Lord, thank You for bringing my brother through surgery without pain, but he doesn't know it was You who did that for him. I tried to tell him, but it went right by him. I'm not even sure Jim realizes it was You answering my prayer. I'm the only one who seems to see it, but even I thought it was crazy when I said it. So, how did it happen?" That's when I realized that God was teaching me effectual prayer; He gives me the words, I speak them out, and He does the work. So simple. And now that I've seen how it works, I want to see more!

Later that year, the Lord pointed out something I hadn't thought to pray for, perhaps because I didn't think God did those things. The one thing I couldn't catch onto as the tech at Bible study was setting the sound volumes for the worship team. From what I understood, I should be able to hear who is singing the melody and harmony and adjust the soundboard sliders accordingly. But for some reason, I couldn't seem to get it right. Neither could the others on my team. To help us, the worship leader started including notes with the lyrics of who would be singing the melody so I'd know to turn that mic up. I did my best, but judging by their rising level of frustration, it wasn't working out as planned. I felt awful but didn't know what to do about it. Finally, I went to God with it and said, "Lord, what should I do?"

The answer came Sunday during the sermon at church. While the pastor was talking about harmony in the body of Christ, I heard that I should let the Holy Spirit set the volume levels. My first thought when I heard it was, *But how would He move the sliders on the...?* Then, in the middle of my thought, I remembered, "Oh yeah, God can do all things." Excited about how it would happen, I said, "Ok, Lord, do it! You set the sound levels!" So, on Friday, during the sound check, I thought we'd see the sliders move by themselves. But another tech got to the soundboard first and set the volumes.

When I tweaked them a little, we immediately looked at each other and knew it sounded great! At the end of the morning, we got compliments from the worship team and others who came by the sound booth to tell us how good the music sounded. I took it all as confirmation from God that He had set the sound levels. It was further confirmed the following year when guest musicians came to sing Christmas songs. After their performance, the drummer's father told me we'd done a good job setting the sound volumes. His compliment meant even more to me when he added he was a retired soundman and listed a few big-name sound stages where he'd worked, which included Disney. I relaxed after that, believing God must be pleased to have sent a professional to encourage me.

So, after pondering my friend's question, I still think "The Greater Life" is a destination, and I think I'll recognize it when I get there. It'll be where I'll see happen what Jesus talked about in John 14:12: "Most assuredly, I say to you, he who believes in Me, the works that I do he will do also; and greater works than these will he do, because I go to My Father." I admit my motivation in seeking "The Greater Life" may not always be to please God. I want to see people healed when I pray. I want to know what it's like to feel the power of God come through me. I want to experience what Jesus said I would in John 14:12. And I believe the Lord is leading me there from what I learned at Reflection Creek. What the Lord taught me when I prayed before my brother's surgery was a huge step toward it—He gives me the words to say, I say them, and He does the work. So simple! And He slipped those words to me without realizing it was Him until I thought about it. I didn't know how God set the sound volumes, and I still don't. But now that I've seen God do things I hadn't even thought to pray for, I want to see more like it and even greater things.

39 PARADE PARK

My lessons on prayer and pondering continued when something happened after serving in our church's tent at the city's annual parade and festival. It seemed to be the start of experiences to bring about the healing miracles I'd wanted to see.

As people filed into the park after the parade, Jim and I were ready with games, prizes, and treats for the kids. We also answered questions about our church and offered literature to those interested. After our shift, we strolled through the park, checked out some other activities, looked through the classic cars on display, and selected something for lunch from among the many vendors. With our lunch in hand, we spotted a couple of available seats at a picnic table with two other couples. When we asked if we could share their table, they politely welcomed us. Nothing more was said while we ate until one of the couples got up and left, and a woman and two young men quickly took their place. They immediately began a conversation with the other couple and us. When one said, "Can I ask you a question?" my first thought was that it would be about God, and I suspected the other couple thought so too. It did turn out to be about God, but not at all what I was thinking. They asked if there was anything they could pray about for us. Before Jim or I could say anything, the other couple asked if they were from a church. When they named their Christian church, the woman asked for prayer for her husband's spinal stenosis. The three, in turn, prayed for Al, asking the Lord to heal his spine and shower Al with His love and blessings.

After the prayer, we chatted, waiting to see Al's healing. The ones who prayed asked why we were all there. Al and his wife said they had lived down the street for 59 years and always enjoyed the annual parade and festival. When I said that Jim and I were there helping in our church's tent, they asked if we had prayed for people there. No, I said, we were so busy playing games and answering questions, I didn't think to ask, but we definitely should have. They shared that they wanted to see miracles and decided to go out and pray for people. They said this was their first time and that it was scary. I encouraged them by saying what a great job they were doing. I sat amazed at how they went about it and how appreciative Al and his wife were that they had prayed for him. We all wanted to see a miracle for him. I also found it interesting that while I'd wanted to see miracles, these young people stopped by and showed me how to do it.

Another opportunity presented itself a few months later, during our early Valentine's dinner. While waiting for our meal, two couples were seated at the table across from us. After observing them for a few minutes, I surmised they were two sisters with their husbands. Spontaneously, I told them how I had them figured out. The ladies laughed and said the guys were lifelong buddies with their wives. One added that they were there celebrating the other couple's 50th wedding anniversary.

A few minutes later, the manager came to their table. I heard him say, "Do you want me to call 911?" They said, "Yes," and the manager quickly went away. From what I overheard, it seemed the woman celebrating her anniversary was having a possible stroke. I silently started praying for her. A few minutes later, four paramedics with a gurney came between our tables. They checked out the woman, and then I heard one say to the other, "There's weakness on the entire left side." Then, they lifted the woman onto the gurney. I was tempted to reach out my hand and pray in Jesus' name, but I didn't. As they were leaving, the other couple apologized to Jim and me. I told them not to worry about us and that we were praying for their friends and them. She thanked me and said they had just returned from a three-week cruise celebrating their anniversary. I continued to pray as they came to my mind for the rest of the night.

The following morning, they were still on my mind. It bothered me that I didn't touch the woman and say a quick prayer while the gurney was right in front of me. I regretted missing that opportunity to exercise my faith and save a life. While micing the teaching director at Bible study, I shared what had happened at dinner the night before and about regretting not laying hands on the woman and praying for her in the restaurant. Sharon said she knew me, and I would have acted if God had prompted me. I wasn't as sure and confessed to her that I thought the fear of looking foolish may have kept me from responding. She understood but insisted I would have acted if I was sure it was right. Although I loved that she said she knew me and believed I would have acted if God instructed, I still wasn't so sure. But decided to think of it as a learning and growing experience.

Later, I shared the story and what the teaching director said about it with my worship leader friend. Her response was similar: "I sure understand how fear can take over and keep us quiet. And even though that may have been part of the equation, I think Sharon is right. If God had truly needed you to reach out and speak out, He would have made it so clear that the fear would have been overpowered. Sometimes His work is done in quiet, faithful prayer." She also agreed with me that God was using it as a learning and growing experience and was praying God would use it to grow us both.

In previous lessons, I learned how God could work through me without realizing it. So, did He this time also? Could my mistake be in second guessing what I did? Were my friends right that I would have acted if God had prompted me? Or had I ignored God's prompting out of fear? I still wasn't sure. Nor could I be sure God hadn't acted on my silent prayers to heal the woman. What I was sure of was that I was learning. I'd learned from strangers that prayer is appreciated and makes people feel loved. By confiding in trusted

Christian friends who know me, I'd learned some about myself and that they, too, can grow from my experiences. So, the lesson from Parade Park is to keep learning and growing. As my journey continued, I discovered how clearly God can communicate and get me to act on His prompting. I'll share that next.

40 VIRTUAL ISLAND

My lessons on learning and growing were turned up a couple of notches when a national emergency suddenly changed everything. As the world looked to technology for ways to communicate, not only across the continents but now from across the street at a pace never seen before, my limited technical knowledge was quickly stretched way beyond my comfort zone. An intense spurt of communication with God, or a meltdown before the Lord, as I called it, quickly reminded me that there's still no technology needed to communicate with God. When an answer I received from the Lord gave me a reason to eagerly pursue the challenge, I couldn't resist.

When the church hosting our Bible study suddenly closed because of COVID-19, we were only a few weeks from finishing the year. Wanting to complete the few lessons left in the study, our teaching director asked if I'd come to her house to video her lectures and then upload them to an internet site for the class to view from their homes. Though we'd talked about adding video to our audio recordings, I hadn't yet looked into it. But when the tech on my team said we could borrow her daughter's video camera, I gave myself a crash course on how to use it by reading the manual, and off I was to video the teaching director. I also went to the home of the scheduled opening speaker and recorded what she had to share. The worship leader recorded herself singing and playing guitar, with her phone and sent me the file via an internet transfer site. Transferring large files was the one thing I was already familiar with from my graphics business. I also discovered my computer had come with video editing software, and I learned how to use it by watching YouTube videos. I found out I could learn just about anything on YouTube, including how to upload videos to YouTube. I even learned how to overlay the lyrics on the song videos so the ladies could sing along at home. The children's ministry also started telling their Bible stories to the kids via video and sending them to me to upload with the others. As happy as we were to be able to complete our lessons for the year this way, we were all looking forward to being back together at the church in the fall for our next study.

During the summer break, when it didn't look like the church would be reopening in the fall, the teaching director began looking to the Zoom video conferencing internet platform as a way for our class to be together. I was glad to hear others in the leaders' group were counseling her because I knew nothing about Zoom. Once she decided to conduct our class on Zoom, I got a call and was asked if I'd be the Zoom tech. I thought she'd be better off with those already involved who knew Zoom, so I first said, "No," but afterward, I felt really guilty. As happy as I was not to do it, at the same time, I felt like I was letting the teaching director down. And the thought of letting God down seemed too much to bear, which brought on my meltdown before the Lord. I started listing all the things throughout my journey with God that had taken me way out of my comfort zone. In a highly frustrated tone, I said, Lord, "I've learned all that tech stuff: the soundboard, adjusting microphones for the music team, PowerPoint, and operating the screens. I learned how to teach the children Bible stories. I even took singing lessons! And now Zoom?!" After getting it all out, I calmly said, "I just want to be left alone and write my book." Then I heard His quiet voice in my heart say, "This is your book." How could I say no to that? So, I decided I would do whatever I was asked to do if I was asked, which I was.

Before the new study year began, we were asked to think of a word we would want the other leaders to pray for us and to be prepared to say the word aloud in our first meeting. The plan was to write down the one-word prayers as we heard them and then pray throughout the year for each one to receive them. I spent the week trying to think of a word but didn't have one until I was called upon to say my word. Then it came to me... Able. I told them, "I just want to be able to fulfill my ministry duties and to have the ability to do what's needed."

As it turned out, Zoom was easier than going to people's houses to video them. I could record directly on Zoom, and the files were saved on my computer. Singing and playing guitar didn't sound well on that platform, though. So, the worship leader continued recording herself and sending me the video to play on Zoom. When she started missing the other two she usually sings with, we met at her house so I could video them together and then played the video on Zoom, which worked out pretty well.

There came a time when I realized how much I was responsible for and began to worry about what they would do if I couldn't start the class for some reason. What would happen if I were to get sick or even if I had computer trouble? I started thinking I should have a backup, someone they could go to. I checked with my tech teammates and was told one was recovering from major surgery, and the other was busy with family needs. So, I went to God for help and asked, "Lord, what am I going to do about a backup?" He answered me with a simple question that had me questioning my faith. He said, "If I'm enabling you, why would you need a backup?" After that sunk in, I thought, *Yeah, why would I need a backup if God is enabling me?* So, I continued doing everything I was asked to do. I started to relax and even began to get creative. I learned how to do a funny video with a countdown timer that cued the worship leader to start us off by introducing the song. Hearing the ladies' reactions to my video countdown encouraged me to do even more.

Then, one night, I had a dream, that I believed, was telling me things had changed and it was time to have a backup. I dreamt I was at my cousin's house, a house I hadn't ever been to, either in my dream or real life. It was a large house, and I had slept there overnight.

When I woke up, there was no one there. I went from room to room and found myself alone in this house. When I looked at the clock, it was almost time for me to start the virtual Bible study class. I looked around for my purse, and I couldn't find it. I had no keys to drive home where my computer and everything were set up to start the class. I didn't even have my phone to call and tell someone I couldn't begin the class. It seemed so real, but when I woke up, I was relieved that it was just a dream and that I hadn't missed Bible study.

After thinking about it, I couldn't remember the last time I had a dream, especially one I could remember so clearly. I even told Jim about it. Could God be telling me it was time for a backup? That question was answered soon after the dream when the timing of something else I'd long awaited coincided with the last class of the year, which meant I would need a backup. I'll tell you about that next.

41 DECISION ROW

After three years of delays, including the court being closed due to COVID-19, the trial of the drunk driver responsible for my brother's death and two others came down to a plea deal. Instead of a trial, there would now only be the sentencing. When the sentencing date landed on the last day of our virtual Bible study class, I struggled with deciding whether or not to go, along with a few other things. Little by little, in the weeks ahead, it all got worked out.

I could have run the virtual class from our motel room on my laptop computer if the sentencing hadn't been scheduled simultaneously. They were both to be on the same day and at the same time, more than 500 miles apart. Once I got past my initial question of, "Couldn't it have waited one more week after all this time?!" the big question was, "Should I go or stay?"

Though it wasn't what I wanted, it seemed apparent I should stay since there was no one to run the virtual Bible study class but me. The district attorney said we could be there and speak, or we could send a letter that the judge would read. It seemed sending the letter was the way to go.

When I told the teaching director at Bible study the sentencing date, she said if I wanted to be there, they would be okay, and she even encouraged me to go to have closure. She also prayed for God to guide my path and told me to pray hard. I wasn't so much concerned about having closure, though; I wanted to go and represent my family, hoping to impress on the court that what they did there mattered very much to us. So, I prayed hard. I also sent in my Victim's Impact Statement for the judge to read if I couldn't attend.

While updating friends on how the trial had turned into the sentencing, one friend commented that I would finally be able to tell the defendant I forgave her. That was a scary thought for some reason. It made me wonder if I had truly forgiven her. I thought I had, but now, with the fear of looking her in the eye and telling her, I wasn't so sure. I wanted to read my Victim's Impact Statement in court, the one the Lord had given me soon after my brother's death, back in Courage

Ridge. But now, having an actual date, it had become more real. Would I have the courage to face her and the hurting families who may not understand or even think it's right to forgive someone who recklessly killed our loved ones? I didn't know, but I trusted it would work out.

When Jim and I arrived at church Sunday morning, I noticed our lay pastor, who is also a Superior Court judge. As I passed him, I thought he would be good to talk to. But he was already talking with someone, so I didn't. Then, after the service, while Jim and I were walking to our car, we came upon the judge in the parking lot. Seeing it as my opportunity from the Lord, I stopped him and said I wanted to ask him a question, which he welcomed. I asked, "How does it work with God if I forgive someone but still want them prosecuted for their crime?" He explained that if a drunk driver almost kills you, they need to know they did something wrong, so they aren't allowed to go out and do it again and possibly kill someone. When he asked if that helped me, I said, "Yes." Then I told him how interesting it was that his example was similar to my situation. Though the judge helped me know that wanting the defendant prosecuted doesn't nullify forgiving her, I still wasn't sure I could look her in the eye and tell her.

Through trying to figure out if I'd genuinely forgiven her, I admitted to God and myself that I wasn't there yet, which led to a profound moment. I thought maybe it wasn't as easy for God as I'd always assumed. Jesus struggled with something in the Garden of Gethsemane before His crucifixion. Could it have been about forgiving those who crucified him, I wondered. I had no way of knowing, but just thinking about it gave me a greater appreciation for our forgiveness from God. The good news is that Jesus followed through with the actions that proved our forgiveness. Could I confirm that I forgave her by standing up in court and telling her? I still didn't know. Plus, there was still the question of who would run the virtual Bible study class.

While still struggling with my decisions, the Lord finally answered the big question of whether or not to go. In my heart, I heard, "If you would only go and put yourself in that environment, I will do the rest." That I could do, and I felt relieved that was all I had to do. So, I decided to go, and the race was on to train a backup to do my job at Bible study. My teammates were now available and very willing. We all worked hard preparing them to run the class in my absence.

Although I was prepared, I didn't read my letter in

court. I sensed the Lord didn't want me to. Before the sentencing, the district attorney met with the victims' families to review the court proceedings and procedures. He said the judge and the defendant had been given copies of all the letters sent in and assured us the judge had read them at least three times. He thought it would only be redundant if we read the letters to them but said we could if we wanted to. I still wanted to read my letter until he said we could not address the defendant directly and had to read our letters to the judge. Since my statement was written to the defendant, not the judge, I felt it was my cue from the Lord not to read my letter. It was confirmed after the others argued with the district attorney over not addressing the defendant. They thought that's what it was all about. The district attorney sternly explained that was the court's procedure, and he didn't want to do anything that would further delay the case in any way. None of us wanted that! He consoled them by saying they could read their letter to the judge, that the defendant would hear it, and the judge would understand. They were all happy to be able to read their letters, but I was still at peace with my decision not to read mine.

Tears were mixed with anger as they read their

lengthy, very personal letters of how their lives, hopes, and dreams had been destroyed forever. By the end, most in the courtroom were crying, and the judge was crying while she proclaimed the maximum sentence. The district attorney later told us he had never seen that judge breakdown like that. I thought that may have been God working. I also saw a sign that God may have been working in the defendant. Her attorney read a letter of apology that she had written. She took responsibility for her actions and apologized for everyone's pain.

Court went well, and I was glad I was there to experience the closure that came with it. I didn't think it would mean as much as it did. Though I was sad not to have my brother, not having the anger the others had, confirmed that I genuinely had forgiven her. I was left bewildered at what went on at Bible study, though. When God said if I'd go, He would do the rest, I assumed it included Bible study. I'll let you know how that all worked out next.

42 WALL VIEW

I couldn't believe my eyes while watching the virtual Bible study class recording and saw that the music video wouldn't play. Debra, the worship leader, ended up singing the song live a cappella! It was beautiful but wasn't how it was supposed to go. I didn't want to think the Lord had let me down, although it looked that way until He showed me a different way to look at it. I was also given another way of looking at myself.

My tech team did so well during our practice sessions that I was confident they would do well running the virtual class while I was away at the sentencing of the drunk driver who killed my brother. When I asked them why the music video didn't play, they didn't know, only that they both had the same technical issue. Whatever it was, it corrected itself about two-thirds of the way through Debra's song when the video abruptly started. The weird thing is that the video with the three singing took over at the same place Debra was singing. It was so incredible! When I asked my tech team how they managed that, they said, "It just happened!" I couldn't help wondering what the odds of that would be. *It had to be God,* I thought. But if God was there, why didn't He step in sooner? Why didn't He see that the video played as it should have? I didn't get it. Did I not hear Him correctly while deciding to go to the sentencing that, if I'd go, He would do the rest? The answers to those questions came almost a year later.

In the meantime, I tried not to let what happened affect my trust in God, but I figured it had when I had trouble singing a particular song at church. During the part of the song, "You're never gonna, never gonna, never gonna let me down," I would either start crying or stop singing. I didn't want to, but it was evident that I was holding what happened with the video against the Lord. So, I told the Lord, "I don't think You let me down; it only looks that way." I was shown a different way of looking at it the following year at Bible study when we were again meeting in person.

The discussion in my study group was so interesting

that I lost track of time and had to hurry back to the sound booth to start the worship team. On the way, I worried that Debra and her team would start without me. But when I arrived, it was just Debra; the others weren't back from their groups yet. Relieved, I confessed to Debra that I was afraid they would start without me. She looked at me and said, "And we would." I thought it was so funny! I laughed, thinking, how could they start without me? They needed me to turn on the mics and give the signal. After I'd laughed and shared the story with others, including the teaching director, I started thinking more about it. I thought about how amazing Debra is; she knows her purpose and will do it no matter what. I thought about how I knew she'd start without me because she'd done it before—when the videos wouldn't play while I was at the sentencing.

As I remembered and prayerfully thought about what had happened, I suddenly saw that God hadn't let me down. He just had a different plan. When the video wouldn't play, and Debra had to sing, I saw it as a failure. When the video started playing in the same spot where Debra was, I thought it was no coincidence. It was God showing me He was there. Back then, I couldn't understand why God didn't do something.

Now I see that He did! He had Debra sing! He knew she would, and He had her ready! It was so amazing that I shared with our teaching director how God had used the funny story about Debra starting without me to help me understand and heal what happened while I was at the sentencing. When I told her I didn't know why it had taken almost a year, she said it probably took me that long to be ready to receive it. I knew I finally had when the following Sunday at church, I had no problem singing, "You're never gonna let me down!" Later, the Lord showed me another way to view something else that took me a long time to receive.

Jim and I had hired a contractor to extend the top of the block wall in our backyard to keep our dog from jumping to see the neighbor's dog. We hoped they wouldn't bark as much if they couldn't see each other. After Roger had a few blocks on the wall, he asked me to come take a look. The grout lines seemed rough and uneven, and I told him I thought it would look more like he said when we hired him. He said it would, but I wasn't so sure at that point. Our conversation got a little heated, so I decided it was a good time to go for my walk.

While on my walk, I was talking it over with the Lord. I said, "Lord, it's like Roger doesn't see what I see.

It looks messy, but he keeps saying how clean it is. It's like we are seeing two different things." Then the Lord said, "You are." "What? How can that be?" I said. Then He explained that Roger knows his work and sees how it will look when it's finished. Like how I see you, He said. I see you as My finished work, but you see yourself as a work in progress. Suddenly, I understood, and it all made sense how Roger and I saw two different walls! Roger saw it finished, nice and clean, but I was seeing it in progress. My chat with the Lord helped me trust Roger's work, and I knew it would all turn out well. It also told me I needed to start seeing myself as God sees me—as His finished work.

After working it all out in my mind, I felt terrible that I'd given Roger a hard time. He wanted to smooth things out between us when I returned from my walk, so without thinking, I said, "That's okay. The Lord spoke to me, and I know it will turn out well." After saying it, I was afraid Roger might think I was crazy, but I was so surprised when he excitedly said, "Really? What did He say?" So, I told him the whole story. He was grateful that I told him and believed it was a word from the Lord, which confirmed it for me, too. The wall did turn out well, and though it hasn't stopped the dogs from barking at each other, it's been a constant reminder that God sees me as His finished work.

My journey to "The Greater Life" has turned out differently than I initially thought. I thought it would be about doing miracles like Jesus did and even greater, like He told the disciples they would do. Instead, it's mainly been about changing my view of myself to match how God sees me. After thinking more about what God said to me about being His finished work, I realized having the Holy Spirit, the Greater One, in me, enabling me to do great things, is His finished work. I don't know why it took so long, but I now see that's The Greater Life! Thank You, Lord; I'm excited to see what we will do!

ABOUT THE AUTHOR

At age 43, Louise Mueller went to church to help a friend. Surprised that the sermon contained principles she'd learned in self-help books and knowing the Bible was written first, she began attending church and received Christ. Her journey with God started after giving up her plan to take her own life and instead asked God to take her. In her first book, *A Different Way—Journey to a Better Life,* Louise shared her experiences, questions, and the amazing answers she received from God, and the journey continued with this second book, *Precious, Honored, Loved—Journey to The Greater Life.*

By sharing her experiences with God, Louise hopes others will be inspired to ask for their own journey with God.

Louise has been a freelance graphic designer for 45 years. Married to her wonderful husband, Jim, for 28 years. They both are native Californians.

Made in the USA
Columbia, SC
20 August 2024